# WILLIAMS

D0505576

*Other books by this author:*

FIFTY YEARS OF FERRARI
A grand prix and sports car
racing history

FERRARI
The battle for revival

DAMON HILL
On top of the world

WILLIAMS
Triumph out of tragedy

WILLIAMS
The business of grand
prix racing

DAMON HILL
From zero to hero

THE QUEST FOR SPEED
Modern racing car design
and technology

DRIVING FORCES
Fifty men who have shaped
motor racing

# WILLIAMS

## FORMULA 1 RACING TEAM

**Alan Henry**

© Alan Henry 1998

All rights reserved. No part of this book may be reproduced or transmitted in any form or by any means, electronic or mechanical, including photocopying, recording or by any information storage or retrieval system, without written permission from the publisher.

First published in March 1998

A catalogue record for this book is available from the British Library

ISBN: 1 85960 416 1

Library of Congress catalog card no. 97-77754

Haynes North America Inc.,
861 Lawrence Drive, Newbury Park,
California 91320, USA.

Published by Haynes Publishing, Sparkford,
Nr Yeovil, Somerset BA22 7JJ, UK.

Tel: 01963 440635 Fax: 01963 440001
Int. tel: +44 1963 440635 Fax +44 1963 440001
E-mail: sales@haynes-manuals.co.uk
Web site: http://www.haynes.com

Designed and typeset by G&M, Raunds, Northamptonshire.
Printed and bound in France by Imprimerie Pollina s.a., Luçon, France n° 74295

# Contents

# Acknowledgements

Thanks to all those at Williams Grand Prix Engineering, from Frank Williams and Patrick Head downwards, who have been so helpful to the author in his journalistic role over so many years. In particular I would also like to thank Jane Gorard, Ffiona Welford and Lindsay Morle in the team's press office for their unstinting assistance at all times.

Alan Henry
Tillingham, Essex
March 1998

# Introduction

At the end of the day, it fell to Heinz-Harald Frentzen to put the final piece of the jigsaw in place, to achieve the result which rounded off another glittering chapter in the history of Williams Grand Prix Engineering. The scene was the 1997 Japanese Grand Prix at Suzuka and the closing stages of a complex and controversial motor race.

*Frank Williams behind his desk at the Grove headquarters of Williams Grand Prix Engineering.* (Formula One Pictures)

When the chequered flag finally dropped, the genial Heinz-Harald was a mere 1.3sec behind Michael Schumacher's Ferrari. Some people judged it disappointing that he hadn't won. But, for all the frustrations of Frentzen's first season as a Williams driver, it was he who sealed the team's ninth Constructors' World Championship title with that memorable second place.

*Nine* Constructors' Championships. When Frank Williams began running an F1 team in 1969, using an off-the-peg Brabham-Ford driven by brewery heir Piers Courage, nobody could have imagined that he would end up on top of the F1 world.

It had been barely a decade since Tony Vandervell's sleek green Vanwalls had won the first official Constructors' Championship in 1958. Since then, BRM had won it once, Cooper, Brabham and Ferrari twice and Lotus three times. In 1969, Frank's freshman year, the French Matra company would take the title. Throughout the 1970s they would be followed by Tyrrell, Lotus, McLaren and Ferrari. Not until 1980 would Williams win its first such crown.

Yet here at Suzuka, only 17 years later, Williams was celebrating its ninth title. At the end of the day, the statistics say it all for Frank Williams and his team. Since 1973 – when Frank technically became an F1 constructor for the first time – his cars have

*Starting out. Frank's Brabham-Ford BT26A on the way to second place in the 1969 Monaco Grand Prix, driven by his close friend Piers Courage. (LAT)*

contested 379 races with 103 wins, a strike rate of 27.1 per cent.

Key rivals McLaren have appeared in 460 races since 1966 with 107 wins, a strike rate of 23.2 per cent. Old hands Ferrari, who have raced in 587 Grands Prix since 1950, have 113 wins to their credit, a strike rate of 19.2 per cent.

The countdown to the team's ninth Constructors' title ran on a course concurrent with Jacques Villeneuve's aspirations for the Drivers' title. At Suzuka Jacques started the other Rothmans Williams Renault FW19 from pole position in circumstances which were politically difficult, so say the least. During one free practice, the Canadian driver had set his quickest lap while the yellow warning flags were being displayed at a marshal's post to signal that a Tyrrell-Ford driven by Jos Verstappen was parked at a supposedly dangerous spot.

*Turning point. Clay Regazzoni heading for victory in the 1979 British Grand Prix at Silverstone with the Williams FW07. (LAT)*

Not that Villeneuve was alone when it came to this rule infringement. No fewer than four of his colleagues – including his rival for the World Championship Michael Schumacher – were also hauled up in front of the stewards. Unfortunately Villeneuve was already racing under a one race suspended ban for a similar rule violation in the previous month's Italian Grand Prix. As a result, he was excluded from the race.

Williams quickly announced that it would be lodging an appeal against the exclusion, allowing Villeneuve to take up his allotted position on the front row of the grid. What ensued was an overtly tactical race with Villeneuve initially running at the head of the

*Howden Ganley in the 1973 Williams, dubbed the Iso-Marlboro. Grand Prix success was still six years away for Frank's team. (LAT)*

pack, keeping the pace down in the hope that one of the other competitors might elbow his way ahead of Schumacher's Ferrari, thereby perhaps pushing the German driver further down the finishing order.

## *Frank allowed himself a thin grin of wolfish satisfaction*

To that end, he was not worried when Schumacher's team-mate Eddie Irvine surged into the lead at the end of the third lap. Jacques was primarily concerned with Schumacher's whereabouts on the circuit, nothing more. But eventually Jacques's strategic advantage would ebb away, crucial time lost at his second refuelling stop dropping him back to fifth at the chequered flag.

Michael Schumacher won the race, with more than a passing degree of obstructive assistance from Irvine, and went into the final race of the year only a single point behind Villeneuve. That situation would be transformed less than a week later when Williams decided to withdraw its appeal against Villeneuve's exclusion from the Suzuka race, thereby losing the two Championship points earned for fifth place. Now he would go into the final race a single point *behind* Schumacher.

For the moment, however, that was in the future. When Schumacher brought the Ferrari in for its second refuelling stop on lap 33 – with just 20

laps more to run – Frentzen sailed through into the lead. On lap 37 Heinz-Harald duly made his second stop and came back into the race in second place. Now he really piled on the pressure, determined to make Schumacher, his old rival in both love and war, sweat as much as he could through to the finish.

After his second stop, Frentzen picked up the chase 8.5sec adrift. By lap 43, with ten more to run, he was 5.53sec behind and was only 4.44sec away from the Ferrari on lap 47. Then on lap 51 Schumacher lost 2.8sec lapping Damon Hill's Arrows. Helpfully, Damon didn't delay Frentzen by a single fraction, perhaps nostalgically recalling the moment 12 months earlier at Suzuka when he had clinched his own World Championship title at the wheel of a Williams.

Despite straining every sinew, Frentzen couldn't quite get the job done and hunt down Schumacher to take the win. Nevertheless, he sprang from the cockpit of his Williams with a broad grin on his face, warmed by the realisation that he had, in his own small way, written the final paragraph in the latest glittering chapter of the team's history.

Back in the Williams pit there was plenty of hand shaking and back slapping. Patrick Head, the team's technical director, walked among the mechanics, a big smile on his face as he offered thanks and congratulations. Frank Williams allowed himself a

*Grand alliance. Williams (left) with Alan Jones, his team's first World Champion in 1980. (LAT)*

pencil-thin grin of wolfish satisfaction from his wheelchair, but mentally he was already focusing on the next race, the next win, the next Championship.

It was amazing to reflect that Frank had been in that wheelchair – paralysed from the chest down, dependent on others for almost every physical move – throughout all the glory years of his F1 team. True enough, Alan Jones had won the 1980 World Championship and Keke Rosberg followed that up with another title in 1982, but it was not until 1986 that Williams's newly forged partnership with Honda was in top gear.

The year the team won its third Constructors' Championship, Frank wasn't around to see much of the action. Following a road accident in France in the spring of 1986 he spent most of the season fighting for his own survival. Eventually he returned to the pit lane, chair-bound perhaps, but having lost none of his motivation. Or his passionate enthusiasm for Grand Prix racing.

Williams won another Constructors' Championship in 1987 before splitting with Honda. Two years later they forged an engine supply partnership with Renault and, in 1990, Patrick Head's design team was immeasurably strengthened by the arrival of Adrian Newey in the role of chief designer.

Newey's forte was racing car aerodynamics. He had developed his skills working for the March team in the

*Frank with Keke Rosberg. The Finn won the championship in 1982, but joked that Williams 'never forgave him for not being Alan Jones.'* (Formula One Pictures)

specialist world of high-speed Indycar oval racing, then switched to the Bicester-based Leyton House F1 operation. He had a reputation as a man who knew his stuff; pragmatic, calm and slightly reserved, he complemented Head's practical directness.

## After Senna's death Damon underpinned team morale

Williams, Head and Newey forged a golden partnership. Powered by a succession of amazingly reliable and potent Renault V10 engines, their cars propelled Nigel Mansell (1992), Alain Prost (1993), Damon Hill (1996) and now Jacques Villeneuve (1997) to a succession of World Championship titles. Perhaps even more significantly, they also won the Constructors' Championship in all those years – plus 1994, when Michael Schumacher took the Drivers' crown after a controversial collision with Hill in the final race at Adelaide.

The Williams team has never gone out of its way to court publicity, even though there were times when it seemed as though its diplomatic skills were somewhat less than fully developed, to say the least. The team lost Nigel Mansell's services at the end of the 1992 season after a protracted debate over the level of his retainer.

No matter, as it turned out. Alain Prost joined the team in 1993 and duly bagged his fourth World Champion-

ship title. But at the end of that season Prost decided to retire from driving after it became clear that Williams was hell-bent on signing Ayrton Senna – the Frenchman's own personal nemesis – for 1994.

Ayrton had first sampled F1 power when Frank invited him to test Keke Rosberg's Williams FW08C at Donington Park in 1983. From then on, the team chief was convinced that Senna had what it took to make the F1 big-time. Yet somehow they never managed to get it together. Either Williams was in the middle of an existing driver contract when Ayrton was available, or vice versa.

In 1993, they finally struck a deal. That would of course end in tragedy when Senna's Williams FW16 crashed at Imola in 1994. His death left the Williams team bereft and the entire international motor racing community mourning the loss of one of its brightest stars of all time.

More anguish was to follow. After a protracted examination of the wrecked car, the Italian authorities decided that the accident had probably been caused by a pre-impact failure of the Williams's steering column. Frank, Patrick Head, Adrian Newey and three race officials were charged with involuntary manslaughter.

In October 1997, the investigating magistrate Maurizio Passarini recom-

*Partners. Patrick Head and Frank Williams have been in business together for more than two decades, the longest-standing partnership between technical director and team owner in F1 history. (Formula One Pictures)*

mended that Williams should be acquitted of any charges in relation to the Senna accident, but Head and Newey remained under the legal microscope. Finally, two months after Frank's acquittal, judge Antonio Constanzo delivered his verdict on the team's technical director and former chief designer, who had been accused of 'badly designing and executing' a modification to the steering column. They too were acquitted of all charges.

In the three and a half years which separated Senna's 190mph disaster from this verdict, Frank Williams and his colleagues had kept the personal pain to themselves. Portrait photographs of Senna in Frank's private office, and in the team's motorhome at the races, served as the only obvious mementoes of what was already a warm mutual regard and might have become one of the greatest racing partnerships in Formula 1.

Second-guessing the future is a futile task at the best of times, particularly in a business as unpredictable as Formula 1. Yet if Senna had survived, it is not beyond the bounds of possibility that he could have won four straight World Championships at the wheel of a Williams-Renault. Had he done so, Damon Hill and Jacques Villeneuve might only have been brief footnotes in motorsport history.

As it was, Damon helped underpin the morale of his Williams colleagues when they were devastated with grief.

*Unrealised potential. Ayrton Senna, (left) with team engineer David Brown, signed for Williams at the start of 1994, only to be killed in the San Marino GP. (Formula One Pictures)*

He would win the Championship in 1996 only to be replaced by Heinz-Harald Frentzen. The validity of this decison was still being pondered by F1 insiders a year after Damon's departure from the team. Perhaps 1998 will enable Frentzen to display the talent many believe he has, yet which was not always burningly obvious during the season just past.

●  ●  ●  ●

Another Grand Prix, another new set of technical regulations. But one thing that isn't planned to change is the Williams team's stranglehold on the World Championship.

That was the upbeat message delivered by Britain's top F1 entrant on 28 January 1998. The venue was a crowded pit lane garage at Silverstone, the occasion a characteristically unobtrusive launch of the latest Williams FW20 challenger.

Not for Williams the strobe lights, dry ice and razzmatazz of the Royal Albert Hall, no Spice Girls, no Sicilian architecture as the backdrop – unlike some of their more extravagant rivals. Just a car, the team personnel and drivers Jacques Villeneuve, the 1997 World Champion, plus team-mate Heinz-Harald Frentzen. And a focused view as to just how they planned to defend the last year's title.

'I think we go into the new season as the team to beat,' said Patrick Head, the Williams technical director. 'I am confident that we can be the principal challenger for the championship in 1998.'

He also expressed the view that Villeneuve is out to overturn the perception of Michael Schumacher as the best driver in F1 today. 'Jacques is very confident and controlled. The general view is that he's a very good driver, but not in Schumacher's class. He wants to put that right. He wants to show either that he is in Schumacher's class, or better.'

Key rivals Ferrari and McLaren might hold out high hopes for their new cars, but the Williams top brass believed the FW20 would start the 1998 Australian Grand Prix, first race of the season, by drawing on more accumulated experience of the new narrow-track, grooved tyre regulations than the other teams.

'I am not particularly enthusiastic about the new rules,' said Head. 'I don't think this is the right way to go. I think that limiting downforce and giving us some nice big tyres, so that the cars could be thrown around a bit, would have been a better way. But these are the rules we have, and it's a question of who is going to do the best job with the regulations as they are.'

There was also a quiet sense of mischievous satisfaction that Ferrari seemed to have squandered its apparent four week advantage. Despite having tested its new F300 before Christmas, it was still experiencing a succession of technical problems with the machine on which Michael Schumacher's title hopes are pinned. Testing at Jerez, the new Ferrari completed only a handful of laps before suffering an engine bay fire and problems with the throttle system and gearbox.

The new Williams – re-liveried from the famous blue to Winfield red – ran

*Jacques Villeneuve and Heinz-Harald Frentzen with the 1998 challenger, all in Winfield red.* (Formula One Pictures)

16 laps of Silverstone in Villeneuve's hands without a mechanical glitch. No representative laps times were set: this was merely an exercise to establish that its wheels would turn and its Mecachrome V10 – formerly Renault – engine would run satisfactorily.

By mid-afternoon the sleek new F1 challenger was being loaded up into the transporter as the team prepared to journey back to the factory. There it would be stripped down again and reassembled with painstaking care, then loaded up and shipped off to Barcelona's Circuit de Catalunya for the first crucial round of pre-season testing.

Frank Williams just smiled, mirroring the confidence displayed by his two drivers. The proof of this particular pudding would be in the eating. For now it was time to look ahead. To Melbourne, Barcelona, Buenos Aires, Silverstone, and Suzuka. All places where motor racing history is made. And where, he hoped, a record tenth crown would be won.

# Chapter 1

# The man behind the team

'There were times when Frank was so hard up that I don't think he was able to pay his tailor's bills.' Excuse me? The assembled group around the table stopped talking and stared at Jackie Stewart. Tailor's bills? This is motor racing, for heaven's sake. Who ever worried about sharp dressing?

The venue was a pit garage at Silverstone on the Friday immediately following the 1997 European Grand Prix. Jackie and Paul Stewart were taking a trip down memory lane with some turns at the wheel of their new F1 team's Stewart-Ford SF1s. Surely, somebody suggested, the 1997 F1 season for Stewart was just the same as the 1969 season had been for Frank when he was running his own private Brabham-Ford for Piers Courage.

'No, not at all,' said Stewart with mock seriousness. 'The difference is that I've always been able to afford my tailor. And we went to the same one – Doug Hayward in Mount Street,

London. Probably the best tailor in London. Frank, you'll remember, seldom wore suits in the early days, but his sports jackets were always a fantastic cut.'

Indeed they were. Frank Williams always had a sense of style. Old sweats who worked for his stumbling F1 operation in the early 1970s remembered that he had a taste for expensive cashmere pullovers. Yet, paradoxically, he was never a poseur. After I had suggested as much in a *Motoring News* Grand Prix report in late 1974, he wrote back briskly:

'For your information, AH, I'm not in F1 just to ponce round the pit lane as a no-hoper. I'm trying to get a serious job done on not much money.' I took the admonishment quite seriously and wrote back a craven letter of apology. It seemed to do the trick.

Francis Owen Garbett Williams was mad about cars from an early age. The son of an RAF officer who split from his mother when Frank was a young kid, he clearly developed a sense of self-contained independence from his youth. 'My mother skimped and saved to give me a decent education and I'll always be happy for that,' he reflects. 'In the end, I was the one who left home to follow my own life.'

## I knew I would eventually have a big accident on the road

Born on 16 April 1942 in South Shields, Frank grew up on Tyneside, but his mother's selfless endeavours enabled him to be educated at St Joseph's College, Dumfries. 'This was Ecurie Ecosse country,' he says, recalling the famous Edinburgh-based racing team whose Jaguar D-types won at Le Mans in 1956 and 1957. He read all the motoring magazines, developed an almost encylopaedic memory for road car performance statistics and confessed himself 'virtually speechless with excitement' when offered a ride in a Jaguar XK150S owned by the parents of a fellow pupil.

Young Williams was absolutely determined to find his way into the contemporary motor racing milieu. Trouble was, in those days it wasn't just a question of finding the key to the door – finding the door itself was a major drama. If you couldn't be a driver, then the only other option was to become a mechanic.

In 1964 Frank raced and prepared a crash-repaired F3 Brabham which was owned by Anthony Horsley, nick-named Bubbles for reasons now lost in the mists of antiquity. They lurched round Europe in an elderly American Plymouth saloon. Those were innocent days. Their experiences could have been used as a script for 'Mr Bean goes motor racing.' Frank left the team wallet on the roof of the car on one occasion. That meant they couldn't afford to pay the ferry from Reggio Calabria across to Sicily in order to compete in a race at Enna-Pergusa.

'So we spent four days camped out in the AGIP station at the ferry entrance, surviving only because the lad at the pumps kept us supplied with drinkable water,' remembers Horsley. 'Only when the racers began coming through on their return journeys could we borrow a hundred quid which enabled us to start on the journey home.'

Gradually Frank dragged himself up the motor racing ladder. In 1965 he raced a Cooper-Ford T72 purchased from British private team owner John Coombs, then switched to a Brabham for 1966. In this car he finally managed to score his only international F3 victory, at Knutsdorp, Sweden, on 28 August 1966.

Yet by then Frank had wisely concluded that he wasn't going to make the international front line as a driver, counting himself fortunate to have escaped unscathed when he wrapped the Brabham round a level crossing gate during a race on the wild and woolly Vila Real road circuit in Portugal.

*The man whose cars had achieved 103 Grand Prix wins by the end of the 1997 season.* (Formula One Pictures)

At the end of 1966 he retired to concentrate on his racing car sales business. He missed the taste of competition though, and still drove far too quickly on the public roads. Years after the accident which confined him to a wheelchair, he reflected on its inevitability to the author with a startling candour:

'I regretted giving up racing a lot. In my heart, I still wanted to be a racer for another ten years, perhaps even into the 1980s. I talked seriously with Patrick Head about racing a touring car to get it out of my system, because I knew I was eventually going to have a big accident on the road and, sure enough, I did just that. It was a fact of life.'

This was a deeply perceptive observation, a slice of self-analysis which goes some way to explain why Frank remains almost goggle-eyed with admiration for racing drivers to this day. If you're negotiating with Frank, says a close colleague, don't send in your manager. 'He's not impressed with bag carriers. But if you're a driver, and you negotiate head-to-head with him, it's quite possible that he'll find your demands irresistible.'

Yet back in the mid-1960s Williams had quickly gained a reputation as a shrewd businessman, capable of thinking on his feet and cutting good deals. The 1967 season can now be seen as a pivotal moment in the history of team owner Frank Williams and his racing

*Tragic day. Piers Courage in the Williams de Tomaso during the 1970 Dutch Grand Prix. Later in the race he would be killed when the car crashed in flames. (LAT)*

cars. At the Motor Show 200, a prestigious end-of-season F3 meeting at Brands Hatch, he fielded the prototype 1967 Brabham BT21B driven by Piers Courage.

Piers Courage, born on 27 May 1942, grew up in circumstances that were distinctly privileged compared with Frank Williams's own modest background. Piers, eldest son of the chairman of the Courage brewery group, was educated at Eton, where he met Sheridan Thynne, who was later to become the Williams F1 team's commercial director. Piers's parents wanted him to pursue a career in accountancy before going into the brewery business. He quickly developed other ideas. For his 20th birthday he was bought a Lotus Seven in kit

*Williams re-grouped in 1971, using this Politoys-backed March 711 driven by Frenchman Henri Pescarolo, seen here at Monaco.* (LAT)

form, but it wasn't long before he swapped that for a sports racing car made by Merlyn, the small specialist constructor based near Colchester, about 30 miles from the Courage family home.

Parental opposition to his racing plans immediately ensued. But although Piers tussled with his mother and father, his will eventually prevailed and he joined the nomadic European F3 circus in 1964, he and Jonathan Williams (no relation of Frank) sharing a pair of outdated Lotus 22s.

Courage demonstrated sufficient promise to earn a place in the Team Lotus F3 squad for 1966 – run and largely financed by his pal Charles Lucas, the son of a Yorkshire landowner – and quickly established himself as one of Britain's most promising young drivers.

In 1967, Piers was invited to drive on a part-time basis for the BRM team, sharing a third car with Chris Irwin. He also drove an F2 McLaren for John

*Arturo Merzario scored some Championship points for Williams during the dark days of the early 1970s, seen here at Monza in 1974. (LAT)*

*Michele Leclere in the disastrous Wolf-Williams FW05 in the 1976 Belgian Grand Prix at Zolder. Frank would split with Walter Wolf at the end of this season. (LAT)*

Coombs. But he wasn't ready and over-drove madly, crashing too frequently. Coombs was so concerned that he begged Piers to pack up racing 'or you'll kill yourself, I know you will!'

Piers bought the McLaren from Coombs, established his credibility in the Tasman series – a lucrative programme of races in Australia and New Zealand which was really a winter Grand Prix series by any other name – then turned down an offer to replace the late Jim Clark at Lotus, instead choosing to race for Tim Parnell in Grands Prix. He was also racing with Frank in Formula 2. So successful was this latter partnership that in 1969 Frank and Piers decided it was time to

# Frank's own racing career

Frank Williams intended to be a driver, but a terminal shortage of cash seemed set permanently to scupper his chances. Yet somehow he managed to get out onto the circuits, racing a self-prepared Austin A40 in 1962. During this period in his life he attempted to keep body and soul together by working variously as a filling station attendant and a Campbell's soup salesman.

In 1963 he decided to make an even bigger effort to get into motor racing, being swept up as a member of the legendary demi-monde of Formula 3 drivers and hangers-on who made the mid-1960s British racing scene so rich in variety and fascination. Now Frank was going to be a mechanic to Jonathan Williams – no relation – who embarked on a European season with a Merlyn Formula Junior car.

'Frank sometimes stood at the right end of the car,' recalled Jonathan years later when asked for an assessment of his namesake's ability as a mechanic. 'But even then it was clear that he was different. For the rest of us, our main priority was to ensure that the fun times kept happening. But Frank had ambitions. He was always going to be somebody, to make something of his life.'

Later he would race his own F3 Brabham, but soon rightly concluded that his talents lay in management rather than behind the wheel of a single seater. He retired from driving at the end of 1966.

*Frank Williams wrestles with the Cosworth engine of Jonathan Williams's Lotus 22, Solitude, West Germany, 1963.*

*Starting over again. Belgian driver Patrick Neve in the Williams March at the 1977 British Grand Prix. The Saudia identification on the rear wing marked the start of a new era for the fledgeling team.* (LAT)

go Formula 1 racing together. Williams managed to pull a flanker on Jack Brabham by acquiring an ex-works 1968 Brabham BT26 chassis at the end of 1968. The plan was to race that in the Tasman series, but Frank eventually decided to make the logical progression and contest the 1969 F1 World Championship with Piers driving the car.

Much to the annoyance of Jack Brabham, whose works cars ran on Goodyear tyres, the Williams Brabham was contracted to race on Dunlops. Piers really came of age that season, with second places in the Monaco and United States Grands Prix testifying to his burgeoning talent. Frank Williams was now poised on the verge of the F1 big-time. Or so it seemed.

During the course of the 1969 season, Frank met Alessandro de Tomaso, a dynamic Argentine businessman whose marriage to the wealthy American Isabelle Haskell had spawned an ambitious commercial partnership. At the time they were manufacturing Ford-engined high performance road cars – the Mangusta and the Pantera were two of their best-known products – in a bid to challenge Ferrari and Lamborghini in this prestige sector of the market.

De Tomaso had already produced an F2 car which showed a degree of promise, designed by Gianpaolo Dallara who would later go on to become a leading F3 chassis maker in his own right some 25 years later. For 1970, de Tomaso proposed that his company build a new Grand Prix car which Frank should prepare and enter for Piers Courage to drive.

Williams's contribution to the equation would be furnishing the engines, driver and organisational expertise, such as it was. Courage agreed to drive the Cosworth DFV-engined de Tomaso 505, turning down a £30,000 offer to join Jacky Ickx at Ferrari. He stayed with Frank on a nominal £3,000 retainer topped up with another £22,500 by signing to drive for the Autodelta Alfa Romeo sports car team.

Sheridan Thynne put the Williams/Courage partnership into sharp perspective when he remarked: 'Because of Piers's personality as an individual rather than as a racing driver, he found the concept of achieving success with Frank enormously appealing. It was a case of wanting Frank and Piers to show Ferrari and Lotus that they could get the job done. Consequently, Piers was strongly moti-

vated to stay with Frank and have things continue as they had been in the past.'

But the de Tomaso 505 was far from the taut, easy-handling Brabham BT24 which Piers had driven the previous year. Courage struggled from the outset. Frank even asked Jackie Stewart if he would do a few laps in the car in practice for the Silverstone International Trophy meeting, just to provide an objective third party view as to precisely what he'd got Piers involved with.

Considered in the context of 1998 Formula 1, this was the equivalent of Eddie Jordan asking Michael Schumacher if he could take a few minutes off from practising his Ferrari and take a quick whirl in the latest Jordan-Mugen-Honda. It just wouldn't

*Alan Jones in the Williams FW06, Patrick Head's first complete F1 design, making a name for himself and the team in the 1978 Long Beach Grand Prix.* (LAT)

happen. Amazingly, both Stewart and his team boss Ken Tyrrell were willing to oblige on this occasion. Jackie did a handful of laps, giving the car back to Piers with a slight frown on his face. His view was that it could certainly be better.

Gradually the team's efforts improved the de Tomaso, but on 21 June 1970, Piers crashed while running midfield in the Dutch Grand Prix at Zandvoort. The car caught fire and he perished in the inferno. One observer recalls Frank standing in the pit lane after it was all over. Devastated, forlorn, his hopes and dreams torn apart.

'I worshipped the guy,' he later said of Piers. 'He was totally adorable. Everybody you've ever heard of in motor racing turned out for his funeral. Nobody ducked it. And there were plenty of red eyes from the hard guys, I can tell you. It was a very moving event.'

Understandably, de Tomaso's enthusiasm for the project evaporated after the Courage tragedy. The partnership with Williams tottered along to the end of the year, by which time Frank Williams Racing Cars was heavily insolvent. Yet Frank was determined to continue in the quest to establish himself as an F1 constructor.

Progress was slow and often uncomfortable. After spending 1971 running a March 711 for Henri Pescarolo, he bagged £40,000 sponsorship from

*Jones waits for the off with the Williams FW07 in the pit lane at the 1979 British Grand Prix. Patrick Head and Frank Williams stand in the background.* (LAT)

Politoys, the Italian model car makers, in order to build a bespoke F1 chassis. This was ready in the summer of 1972, just as the team moved out of its original cramped premises at Bath Road, Slough, and into a new 5,000sq ft factory on the fringes of Reading.

## Tired engines, tatty cars, and pay drivers made the team a joke

Pescarolo celebrated the Politoys' debut by writing it off in the 1972 British Grand Prix. In fact, the Frenchman crashed Frank's cars rather too frequently for it to be amusing. In 1973 Frank gained some backing from the Iso-Rivolta sports car company and Philip Morris's Marlboro cigarette brand. The new machines were dubbed 'Iso Marlboros' as a result, although in fact they were the first dedicated Williams Formula 1 cars.

Frank struggled along, but his team was always a day late and a dollar short. A succession of tired engines, tatty racing cars and second-rate drivers purchasing rides with personal sponsorship that often failed to turn up all conspired to turn Frank's team into something of a joke.

The late Denis Jenkinson once told me he'd said to Frank: 'Why don't you give up F1 and drop down to F2? You could be king there.' Apparently Williams replied robustly: 'No, Denis. I want to make the big-time in F1. It's my ambition to be like Ken Tyrrell.'

By 1975 Williams was on his uppers. The team's phone was cut off so frequently that Frank often had to discuss his business deals from the paybox outside Reading speedway track. Then by chance, an old association yielded a promising steer.

Gianpaolo Dallara was now working for Lamborghini and tipped off Frank about a very rich customer who kept telling them that he wanted to race a Lamborghini at Le Mans 'whatever it costs.' Frank's commercial antenna went onto red alert, reasoning that here might be a welcome sugar daddy to save his own team from collapse.

Walter Wolf was an Austro-Canadian millionaire who had made his fortune in the oil equipment world. But the fact that he was mad on cars and motor racing only partly concealed an astute business mind. After meeting Frank he initially agreed to pay for some engines, but then pressed to purchase a stake in the company.

Eventually Frank capitulated. He sold 60 per cent of Frank Williams Racing Cars to the newcomer and the team was reincarnated as Walter Wolf Racing at the start of 1976, purchasing the rubber-suspended Hesketh 308C project after the English aristocrat closed down his F1 team at the end of 1975.

Unbelievably, things got worse. The 1976 season turned out to be an even bigger disaster than the previous year. The cars were hopelessly uncompetitive and Frank found himself reduced to the role of Walter's highly paid aide-

*Frank Williams on the pit wall.* (Formula One Pictures)

de-camp. This wasn't the way he'd envisaged it all working out.

At the end of 1976 Frank decided to go it alone. The partnership was dissolved, Wolf completely reorganised the team, signed Jody Scheckter as his number one driver and went on to finish second in the 1977 World Championship. Frank rented a small factory unit on an industrial estate in Didcot, purchased a second-hand March 761 and started from square one with a pay driver, the young Belgian Patrick Neve.

---

## The bottom line was that Honda was determined to start winning

---

The new company was named Williams Grand Prix Engineering. More significantly, Frank attracted a young Wolf team engineer called Patrick Head to work on the car. Although neither could have imagined it at the time, this was the start of one of the most spectacular partnerships in Grand Prix motor racing history.

In 1978, Frank signed Australian Alan Jones to lead the team. He'd won the previous year's Austrian Grand Prix at the wheel of an uncompetitive Shadow DN8, but quickly developed into a rugged and determined racer. His best result in 1978 was second place to Carlos Reutemann's Ferrari in the United States GP at Watkins Glen. By this time Williams had pretty much exorcised depressing memories of earlier failures. His team was now fully competitive and taken seriously by rivals in the pit lane.

In 1979, Head produced the first ground-effect Williams FW07, effectively taking the concepts pioneered by Lotus boss Colin Chapman one step further. That year saw Williams eclipse Lotus as a competitive force and Clay Regazzoni won the team's first Grand Prix at Silverstone. Eighteen years later, Jacques Villeneuve would post Williams's 100th victory in the very same event.

Alan Jones followed Regazzoni's success by winning the German, Austrian, Dutch and Canadian races. Jody Scheckter won the Championship for Ferrari, but in 1980 Williams was the dominant F1 force and Jones strode convincingly to the team's first World Championship. In 1981 team driver Carlos Reutemann only narrowly lost the title to Brabham-mounted Nelson Piquet, but Keke Rosberg became the second Williams World Champion in 1982.

In the early 1980s, the fabric of Formula 1 was changing dramatically. Ever since Frank's first F1 foray with Piers Courage in 1969, his cars had been powered by the Cosworth DFV which was commercially available over the counter from the famous Northampton-based race engine builder.

However, in 1977 Renault arrived on the scene with the very first 1.5-

*Jones straps himself into the cockpit of the Williams FW07B for the 1980 British Grand Prix, which he won. (Formula One Pictures)*

litre F1 turbocharged engine, signalling a major change in technical direction. Ferrari followed suit for 1981 and it quickly became clear that not only was this the direction every team would be obliged to follow, but support from a major international motor manufacturer was going to become an increasingly essential element in the equation for any F1 team which hoped to be competitive.

Williams examined the options in detail. It could become a customer for Renault's powerful V6, pursue a deal to use the four-cylinder production based BMW turbo or even consider using Matra's planned V6 turbo. In the end, the team turned to Honda, the Japanese company which was in the throes of developing its own twin-turbo V6 based on a development of its existing Formula 2 engine.

Negotiations with Honda originally began in April 1981 and the deal was not finally confirmed until 22 February 1983, later to be made public in a joint announcement by Williams and Honda's competition chief Nobuhiko Kawamoto at that year's Austrian Grand Pix.

What followed was certainly not an easy ride. Patrick Head found himself building the first Williams turbocar round a lumpy, untidy 80-degree V6, the first example of which arrived at Didcot in a box together with two turbochargers. And that was all. Key ancillaries such as radiators and plumbing for the turbos and exhaust systems were left for Williams to develop pretty much on their own.

'We welcomed Honda working with us at Didcot, because it led to close and worthwhile co-operation,' said

*Jones in 1981 with his chief mechanic Wayne Eckersley, a fellow Australian.* (Formula One Pictures)

Williams. 'For sure, they could be difficult to deal with, but they were nice people and could also be fun. Understanding precisely what they meant could sometimes be a problem and they were often very forthright. They were tough partners who didn't beat about the bush.

'The Honda mechanics liked us and we liked them. We eventually established good communications at all levels throughout the group. Once you dealt with them successfully, it became extremely rewarding. The bottom line was that they were going to win. There were no two ways about it.'

Into 1985 and Patrick Head came up with the first carbon-fibre composite Williams F1 design, the FW10. With Nigel Mansell joining Keke Rosberg in the driver line-up, optimism ran high. The car was competitive and the team notched up a total of four victories, starting with Rosberg's triumph at Detroit and finishing with three wins in a row at the end of the season, Mansell triumphing in the Grand Prix of Europe at Brands Hatch followed by another win in South Africa, leaving his team-mate to round off the season with victory in the first Australian race at Adelaide.

Williams Grand Prix Engineering was now poised on the verge of the big-time. Its founder was a powerhouse of energy. Ultra-fit and alert, like an over-anxious whippet, he missed not a single detail of his team's activities.

Away from his business desk, Frank was a serious runner long before it was athletically fashionable to be so. David Warren, a keen amateur runner who finished eighth in the 800-metres during the 1980 Moscow Olympics, testifies to this fact with some eloquence. The two men met when Warren was doing promotional work for the Canon office equipment company, a Williams sponsors, and he vividly recalls being invited for a run with Frank on the evening prior to the 1985 San Marino Grand Prix:

---

## *Frank was a powerhouse of energy and superbly fit*

---

'Frank came up and asked me if I fancied "going 10" with him later that evening. I naturally assumed he meant 10 kilometres as we were in Italy, and since we didn't get back to the hotel until about 9.30 in the evening, I figured he would forget all about it and suggest we met up in the bar.

'Not a bit of it. He was down in the lobby, ready to go, in about 10 minutes. And he meant 10 miles. What's more, he was running six minute miles throughout which, I promise you, is serious stuff. That's not jogging by any means. Believe me, he was superbly fit.'

Yet on Saturday, 8 March 1986, this would all change. Frank Williams's life would be upended into a physical turmoil that he would be forced to confront for the rest of his life. On that fateful Saturday afternoon his rented Ford Sierra plunged off a secondary road into a field between Le Camp and Brignoles, just inland from the coast at Bandol, in southern France. He was returning to Nice airport after the new and very promising Williams FW11 had completed its final pre-season test session in the hands of Mansell and the team's latest recruit Nelson Piquet.

Williams was travelling with his team manager Peter Windsor at the time. They slid off the road and dropped about six feet into a field. Most of the impact was taken on the windscreen pillar on Frank's side of the car and, from the very moment the car ceased its crazy gyrations, it was clear that Frank had been badly hurt. He could sense all feeling draining from his body.

Frank was initially transported to the hospital in nearby Toulon, then to a better equipped hospital in Marseilles. The FIA's medical supremo Professor Sid Watkins quickly arranged for him to be transferred to the London Hospital and Bernie Ecclestone, president of the F1 Constructors' Association, made available his private jet to bring Frank home.

Ahead of Frank lay months of treatment and painful therapy, none of which could alter the fact that he was now paralysed. Meanwhile, the Williams-Hondas went off into battle, winning a total of nine out of 16 Grands Prix during 1986 as well as the Constructors' title. Yet the boss would not return to the pit lane for almost another year, by which time his company was facing a complex chal-

*Jones dominated the 1981 Monaco Grand Prix until fuel pick-up problems intervened, handing victory to the Ferrari of Gilles Villeneuve. Sixteen years later Gilles's son Jacques would become the latest in a line of Williams World Champions.* (Formula One Pictures)

lenge from an altogether unexpected quarter.

Honda was deeply concerned about the effect Frank's accident would have on his company. Unwittingly, Williams Grand Prix Engineering had now come up against one of the idiosyncracies of Japanese business practice. In their view, there has to be an established and identifiable management framework. Honda could not understand that Williams could function as a company without Frank at its helm on a day-to-day basis.

'At the first race he visited after Frank's accident, Kawamoto asked Patrick and me who was going to run the company,' recalls Sheridan Thynne. 'They couldn't see there wouldn't be a problem, and that we actually didn't need a replacement managing director.

'In Japanese companies, the managing director has what might be described as a well-defined, if symbolic, public relations and promotional role. In their view, you can't have a company without one. The fact that

*Mansell and Piquet with Frank Williams. This duo raced each other's wheels off in 1986/7.* (Formula One Pictures)

we were winning most of the races was ignored. They just wanted us to get a replacement as soon as possible.'

Moreover, despite the Williams team's success in winning the Constructors' title, the Honda top brass was frustrated that neither Mansell nor Piquet managed to secure the Drivers' crown. The Japanese company's founder Soichiro Honda journeyed to Adelaide for the 1986 Australian Grand Prix, confidently expecting one of the Williams drivers to get the job done.

As things turned out, after one of the most remarkable races in recent F1 history, McLaren's Alain Prost dodged through to take his second successive title. Mansell's chances were wiped out by a 200mph tyre failure on the fastest part of the circuit, the Englishman displaying great presence of mind as he wrestled his high tech tricycle to a halt without slamming into one of the concrete retaining walls.

As a result of this failure, Piquet was called in for a precautionary – and, as it transpired, unnecessary – stop to fit fresh tyres. Nelson resumed to finish a fighting second, but it wasn't enough for him to take the Championship either.

Honda had clearly got it into their corporate mind that Frank's disability had compromised the team's strategic capability. In the early months of 1987 they began to make plans to terminate their partnership with Williams at the end of the season, one year short of its contracted term.

It was an uncomfortable time for Williams Grand Prix Engineering, yet somehow Frank's physical plight had endowed him with an even sharper sense of pragmatic clarity. McLaren boss Ron Dennis once said that Frank's disability had given him more time to think – little chance of doing much else, in fact. At the time many people within F1 were shocked at this abrupt assessment. But Dennis was right, and other racing insiders later came to the same conclusion.

It would have been all too easy for Williams to have taken an aggressive legal stance with Honda, but Frank decided against that. Instead he negotiated a financial settlement which gave the team sufficient resources to arrange the use of naturally aspirated 3.5-litre Judd V8 engines for 1988, a rather unpredictable 'interim' season in which turbo and non-turbocharged engines were allowed to exist alongside each other on the F1 stage. For 1989, the turbos would be banned altogether.

---

## *The team owners now faced the downside of this golden egg*

---

The 1988 season was a nightmare for the Williams team. For the first time in a decade it failed to post a single victory. Nigel Mansell then decamped to Ferrari. Piquet had left a year earlier, switching to Lotus for 1988 to continue his relationship with Honda as reigning World Champion.

In 1989, Williams forged a new engine supply partnership with Renault which endures to this day,

*Keke Rosberg scored the first Williams-Honda victory at Dallas in 1984.* (Formula One Pictures)

albeit on a strictly commercial basis from the start of the 1998.

So how has Frank Williams changed over the years since his accident? To the outside world, remarkably little. His absolute passion for racing cars and his company's achievements continue undimmed. He focuses totally on the task of strengthening and enhancing the team's effectiveness. It is therefore no surprise that, after literally years of detailed negotiation, Williams F1 cars will race with BMW engines from the start of the 2000 World Championship season.

If he is frustrated by his physical limitations, by the need for constant nursing care, he never shows any outward sign. Not only are his home and offices specifically adapted to the needs of a quadriplegic, but his company's wealth has enabled him to enjoy the use of a succession of executive jets to transport him to the races.

For many F1 team owners, such multi-million dollar toys are little more than fashion accessories, totems by which they can 'keep score' in the perpetual one-upmanship contest with their rivals. For Frank, a private plane is almost a necessity if he is to attend races the world over.

Williams and his fellow team owners have grown rich beyond their wildest dreams over the past couple of decades, very largely due to the commercial astuteness of Bernie Ecclestone in transforming Grand Prix racing into one of the most successful global televised sports. By the summer of 1997, however, the grandees had to face the downside of this golden egg. Ecclestone wanted to float his F1 Holdings empire on the Stock Exchange. As part of the preparation process, all the competing teams were asked to sign up to a new Concorde Agreement, the complex protocol which governed the way F1 rules were evolved and implemented – as well as deciding what share of the television revenues would accrue to the individual teams.

Ecclestone's faith in the future of 'pay to view' digital television as a means by which to offer viewers dramatically enhanced coverage was an essential element within this proposed equation. But Williams, together with McLaren and Tyrrell, balked at signing up for the new deal.

They felt that Ecclestone was getting too big a slice of the cake and were not prepared to relinquish all their teams' intellectual rights to the sport's governing body which had licensed Bernie's company to exploit the commercial side of the F1 business for an amazing 15 year period. The matter was still only edging towards a permanent solution when this book went to press.

# Chapter 2

# Design and development

Thirty years ago, the design of a Grand Prix car was largely masterminded by a single individual who stamped his own identity very firmly on the finished product. Colin Chapman, the Lotus founder, was typical of this genre. He was a dynamic ideas man whose probing mind came up with a succession of innovative technical developments and solutions.

Whether it was ground effect aerodynamics, monocoque construction or the use of torsion bars as a suspension

*The factory at Basil Hill Road, Didcot, was the team's headquarters from 1984 to 1996* (Formula One Pictures), *and showing the half-scale wind tunnel building on the right* (Formula One Pictures). *In 1996 this was transported to the company's new headquarters at nearby Grove.* (Williams)

medium, Chapman was at the very centre of his team's engineering effort. A few hand-picked engineers operated as trusted lieutenants, rounding off the rough edges of his conceptual thinking with a view to their practical application. But he was very much the man in charge.

## You've got to do a solid job to maintain credibility

In the last decade of the 20th century, the process of Grand Prix car design has developed to a level which would be regarded as unimaginably sophisticated and complex, even by the standards of Chapman's final great design, the 1978 World Championship winning Lotus 79. Yet it can perhaps be regarded as an ironic twist of history that the first Patrick Head-designed Williams FW07, the car which earned the team its maiden Grand Prix victory, was in many ways a logical successor to the last technical tour-de-force of Chapman's F1 career.

Head admits that the FW07's design was largely inspired by the ground-effect Lotus, although by the same token he says he didn't fully understand the function of ground effect at that time. F1 technology was accelerating at such a rate that it soon became clear a wind tunnel was one of the team's key priorities for the immediate future.

This realisation came after Patrick had investigated the wind tunnel at London's Imperial College, scene of much of the Lotus 79 aerodynamic development. Williams's first wind tunnel was acquired from Specialised Mouldings, the Huntingdon company which for many years had serviced virtually the entire British motor racing industry in manufacturing bespoke glass fibre body components.

'By the time we acquired the tunnel, it was too late to influence the design of the FW07,' he recalls. 'In fact, the entire aerodynamic design of the car was based on a single week's work in the Imperial College wind tunnel – in what amounted to the first wind tunnel work I'd ever done in my life. Really, I hadn't got a clue what ground effect was all about and I had to think very carefully about the whole project.

'In the early part of my career I got cured of any idea of being egotistical from an engineering standpoint. By that I mean in the sense that one might say "I'm going to prove to the world that my conceptual ideas are better than anybody else's." I think that attitude came about because I saw the damage that can be done to a company if one person over-indulges himself in conceptual ideas that don't work.

'Chapman was such a big figure at Lotus, in complete charge and with an enormous reputation, that he could take a risk like that. But his development of the Lotus 79, the type 80, was a disaster. It went through the whole season with bits falling off and breaking, which is why Carlos Reutemann left them and came to drive for us.

'But while Lotus could arguably afford to take time off for such experiments, if we had endured a year like

48

# Patrick Head, the practical engineer

Patrick Head was born into a world of motor racing and fast cars. His father Colonel Michael Head had been a military attache between 1949 and 1951 in Sweden where he purchased an alloy-bodied Jaguar XK120 directly from the Jaguar stand at the Stockholm Motor Show. Later he would serve as a military advisor to Sir Solly Zuckerman, the chief government scientist, and was also director of fighting vehicles at the army's military base at Chobham, Surrey.

Parental pressure saw Patrick start out to pursue a naval career, but he spent only three months in the Royal Naval College at Dartmouth before buying himself out of the service at a cost of £195, all the money he had in the world at that time. He subsequently followed a convoluted path to an honours degree in engineering from University College, London, raced briefly in a Clubmans sports car and eventually learned the ropes of racing car design with the Huntingdon-based Lola company.

It was when he was interviewed for a job with the Wolf team that he met Frank Williams at a ritzy London hotel. 'Are you prepared to work 24 hours a day to achieve success in motor racing?' asked Frank. 'No,' replied Patrick firmly, 'because anybody who has to do that must be extremely badly organised.' It may not have been quite the response Williams had anticipated, but the new boy's candour certainly struck the right note. He got the job.

*Head and Williams, in conference.* (Formula One Pictures)

*The Williams F1 machine shop. Massive behind-the-scenes investment is a crucial factor for any contemporary Grand Prix team.* (both Formula One Pictures)

that, certainly in our early days, we would have been hard pressed to survive. Granted we had bad years like 1984, but we always managed to produce enough expectation for the following season. I learned early on that you've got to do a good solid job to survive and keep your credibility in this business.'

Forging an engine supply partnership with Renault has proved to be one of the most significant elements in the sustained success achieved by the team. Continuity of engine supply is a matchless benefit, so much so that after Renault withdrew its factory supply of engines at the end of the 1997 season, Williams decided that the best way of bridging the gap to its new partnership with BMW would be to pay the £13 million annual lease fees required to continue using the powerful French V10 engines – now under

the Mecachrome banner – through to the end of 1999.

'We explored other options, yes, but decided that the Mecachrome option was the most suitable,' Head explains. 'We think the Renault engine is very good indeed and see no reason to change for the following two years.

'Anyway we're very happy with the people we work with at Renault and, I'm told, we've raced a considerable number of times, and certainly practised, in 1995 and 1996 with an engine built and dyno-tested at Mecachrome anyway, so it's not such a big change.'

A much larger potential impact on the Williams team's long-term competitiveness for 1998 could prove to be the departure of chief designer Adrian Newey who left at short notice in November 1996 following a disagreement over contractual terms.

After lengthy legal negotiations,

# Adrian Newey, departed aerodynamicist

Adrian Newey's technical credentials are pretty well impeccable. A graduate from Southampton University with a first class degree in aeronautics and astronautics, Adrian was determined to work in motor racing. He joined the Fittipaldi team in 1980, working alongside designer Harvey Postlethwaite, then moved to March, race engineering the Formula 2 car driven by Johnny Cecotto, and designing the 1983 and 1984 IMSA-winning GTP sports cars.

However, it was to be Newey's experience on the aerodynamically challenging Indycar oval tracks which marked him out as an outstanding engineer. Between 1985 and 1987, his March Indycar designs achieved a hat trick of Indy 500 victories, and eventually he made his way into the F1 arena to become chief designer of the Leyton House Grand Prix team in time for the 1988 season.

Newey stayed with Leyton House until the team began to lose its sense of direction, by which time his F1 designs had posted two excellent second place finishes, in the 1988 Portuguese and 1990 French Grands Prix, with Ivan Capelli behind the wheel on both occasions.

Then came the offer from Williams and the first fruits of Newey's labours at Didcot were seen in the undercut nose Williams FW14 at the start of the 1991 season. This spawned the 1992 FW14B which Nigel Mansell used to win the World Championship, Prost's title-winning FW15C of the following year and the FW16, 17, 18 and 19 which have kept Williams in the forefront of F1 ever since.

*Damon Hill talks things through with the chief designer Adrian Newey at the 1996 Brazilian Grand Prix. He went on to win.* (Formula One Pictures)

Newey took over as technical director of the West McLaren Mercedes team at the start of August 1997. He immediately began working on the team's new car for the 1998 regulations which would call for a significantly narrower track and the mandatory use of a new generation of grooved racing tyres.

Head takes a balanced view over the loss of his talented colleague. On the one hand he is quick to acknowledge Adrian's contribution to the 1997 Championship-winning FW19, yet also praises the effort of other key members of the design team, emphasising that no one individual – himself included – is responsible for the overall design.

'It would be completely foolish to say that Adrian's departure happened without any ripple or change,' he concedes frankly, 'but we haven't had any personnel changes of significance apart from Adrian's departure, and I'm not expecting any. All the others have rounded up, sorted themselves out and got on with the programme.

'I would certainly give Adrian a very considerable amount of credit for this car. On the aerodynamics and general layout of the car, Adrian worked with a number of other designers – and he has always been very good about giving them credit as well – but he was their leader in that area, so he has to take considerable credit for it.

'The general shape and concept of the car is down to Adrian, so obviously a lot of people will be interested to see how we get on without him, but I suspect you won't be able to judge that a lot until 1998.'

Looking to the future, Head has high hopes for the engineers on whose shoulders rests the responsibility of sustaining the team's competitive edge: 'Our chief aerodynamicist is a guy called Geoff Willis who has worked with, and alongside, Adrian for the past six years.

---

## *I ensure that the design is one cohesive effort, not an F1 camel!*

---

'He is very experienced and he has obviously contributed in part to the cars we have produced over the past few seasons. Now he is in a central position on the aerodynamic side, and everything I've seen suggests that he's going to do a very good job. Time will tell.'

As far as Patrick's own contribution to the design of Williams F1 cars is concerned, his role has become more that of a technical co-ordinator over the past few years:

'I have always been involved in the hardware like transmissions, upright, brakes and so-on, but basically we've got a very good team of designers who worked very closely with Adrian. Gavin Fisher is now chief designer, and he co-ordinates a very good group of people on the design of the car. But I have to make sure that it is one cohesive effort and that we don't produce F1's equivalent of a camel – a committee car!'

The very nature of Grand Prix racing means that the Williams FW19 was an evolutionary development of the previous year's car. Renault made a huge contribution to its competitiveness by producing a totally revised V10 engine with a slightly wider cylinder vee angle which was fitted lower in the car and consequently required a brand new six-speed transverse gearbox to go with it.

It has frequently been said that Williams is primarily an engineering company whose specialist activity is Grand Prix motor racing. That wouldn't be the case for Frank, the ultimate racer's racer, but it may come close to mirroring Patrick's own bedrock commitment to engineering excellence.

With that in mind, does Patrick miss the challenge of developing such concepts as four-wheel-drive, active suspension and constantly variable transmission – all aspects of racing car design tackled by Williams at varying moments over the past couple of decades?

'Yes, obviously, as an engineer. To me, the engineering function is the most important thing. However, this question is part of a wider debate in deciding what's best for F1 and whether there should be such freedom in the rules that makes the technical content more important relative to the driver.

'I have to say as a motorsport enthusiast, as opposed to an engineer, I don't think it is appropriate that drivers should have anti-lock braking so that they can just stand on the pedal as hard as they can at all times, regardless of whether there's oil or water on the track, and the electronics just sort it all out.

*The autoclave pressure oven in which the carbon-fibre composite Williams F1 chassis are cured.* (Formula One Pictures)

'I don't think it's appropriate that there should be a steering system which corrects before the driver can for incipient oversteer, or whatever, and I think it is right that these things are not allowed. But as an engineer, I have to say they are very interesting.

'Technology is technology, and it's up to motor racing to harness it to best effect.'

## An F1 design is a snapshot of the team's current data

In practical terms, Williams, like every competitive Grand Prix team, has to balance the need for intense research and development work with the requirement for a new car to be ready for the start of the racing season. In that respect, an F1 design represents a snapshot of the team's knowledge at a given moment, a point in the ongoing research and development programme which is effectively frozen, for better or worse, into the car which will carry that team's fortunes across a World Championship programme.

The day never comes when Patrick Head and his colleagues think 'right, that's this year's car completed. Now we will get on with the racing and come back to think about next year's package in August.' With a research and development department running parallel medium and long-term technical developments in conjunction with a self-contained test team, one of the

gambles is how late to leave it before finalising the concept of a new car, at the same time leaving sufficient time to physically build and test it before the first race of the new year.

'I do try to do some hands-on design work on particular aspects of the car,' says Patrick, 'but generally each engineer gets a specific package to deal with. I will usually write a brief for them which outlines the direction I want them to pursue, and why a particular thing is being done. It amounts to a brief as to what we are trying to achieve, but I try to leave them with some scope for putting a little bit of their personal stamp on a component.

'They will then start on the project and periodically we will have meetings as and when necessary. Perhaps one of them will say "I'm a bit stuck on this, can we have a meeting?" There is also occasionally a situation where they say "look, we've examined it and we can't get such-and-such a component through there, or can't do it in the way you have suggested." If I reckon it is possible, I'll take a copy of how far he's gone and have a crack at it myself.

'I suppose I am the only co-ordinator between the wind tunnel, manufacturing process and what eventually happens out on the circuit. I have to link everything together and, hopefully with some accuracy, predict what long-term technical requirements we will need in the future as well as what's needed on the cars for the next few races.'

Wind tunnel development has grad-

*A Williams F1 challenger on display on the factory reception area at Grove.* (Williams)

ually grown in sophistication over the past decade. By 1990, Williams was carrying out aerodynamic development both with quarter-scale models in their Didcot wind tunnel and with 40 per cent models in the University of Southampton tunnel. But by the end of 1991 a totally new 25,000sq ft building was completed to house the team's new bespoke half-scale wind tunnel which has since been transferred to the team's new headquarters at Grove, near Wantage, a mammoth task in itself which required the temporary closure of the nearby A34 trunk road.

'In order to achieve dynamic similarity – that is to say an accurate representation in the wind tunnel of how the car's aerodynamics will behave out on the circuit – the closer you can get to full scale conditions, the less the margin of disparity will be,' says Head.

'Also, each tunnel obviously has a cross-sectional working area and, depending on the amount of blockage caused by the model within that section, you get errors in the result you end up with. This results from the air speeding up as it approaches the blockage, in this case the model. Obviously, when a car is out on the circuit, there is no such restriction to the airflow.'

Once the information from the aerodynamic testing has been assimilated and assessed, the design process starts using a comprehensive computer-aided design/manufacturing (CAD/CAM) facility. Ever since the Williams FW11 of 1986 such systems have been employed in the manufacturing

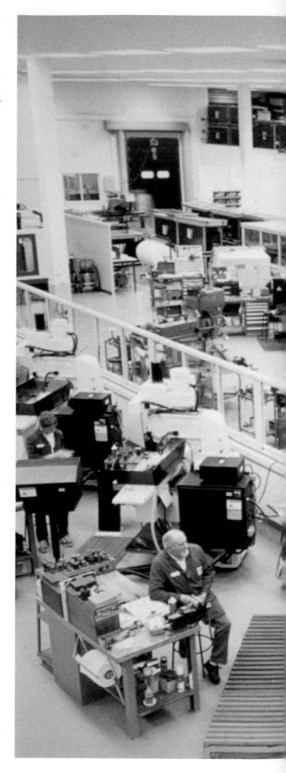

*A general view of the Williams machine shop.* (Williams)

process, enabling hitherto unmatched standards of detailed finish and fine tolerances to be achieved for the installation of all the various components within the outer aerodynamic shell.

The CAD/CAM system enables the technical staff to view and assess the proposed design as a three-dimensional image on the computer screen. In doing so, it is possible to make various amendments to the concept before actually committing the design to the metal. Then further wind tunnel models are made of the relevant car for aerodynamic assessment, subsequent possible modification and then into the build programme for the car itself.

The ability to use CAD/CAM design systems has also led to the areas of finite element stressing which amounts to a detailed structural analysis of complex composite components which go into the development of an F1 chassis. We have already seen that aerodynamics are one of the central keys to a car's effective performance, but the way in which chassis and suspension performance relate to the car's aerodynamic efficiency also calls for tremendous strength and rigidity from the carbon-fibre composite monocoque chassis.

When the first CFC Williams FW10 was constructed in 1985 it was considerably stiffer than its immediate predecessor, the aluminium alloy honeycomb FW09 which Rosberg had taken to victory in the 1984 Dallas Grand Prix. For example, in the cock-

*The spacious race preparation shop, as clean and organised as a hospital operating theatre.* (Williams)

pit area alone there was a 65 per cent increase in torsional stiffness achieved for the same weight of component. It also followed the contemporary trend of the monocoque walls effectively forming the outer bodywork, calling for a complicated moulding which was manufactured in two stages.

With the Grand Prix season starting at the beginning of March, Williams aims to have its new cars ready by the end of January at the latest. This enables them to undergo an intensive test and development programme for about a month before they have to be packaged up and delivered to the appropriate air freight terminal for shipment to Australia which now hosts the opening round of the World Championship.

In this respect, Williams have an easier time than some teams. Its well-honed partnership with engine suppliers Renault has enabled such testing to run smoothly and the evolutionary nature of the team's cars over the past five years have generally ensured that there are few major pre-season problems to be resolved.

Once the season starts, on-going test and development work continues in parallel to the racing effort. There is a dedicated test team which has its own separate mechanics, cars, engineers and supply of engines. For the past two years much of this work has been carried out by Jean-Christophe Boullion who was actually signed up by Williams as test driver at the start of the 1995 season and then hired out to the Swiss Sauber F1 team to race as team-mate to Heinz-Harald Frentzen. It was an unhappy partnership which led nowhere, unfortunately for the young Frenchman.

Boullion won the European Formula 3000 Championship in 1994, traditionally the final step on the ladder for those wide-eyed youngsters who hope to make the final leap into the Grand Prix arena. He still wants to prove that his expertise as a test driver makes him a worthwhile competitive proposition for a full-time drive elsewhere. 'I think I have proved my capability. I am fit and motivated and the discipline of a Williams testing role has helped my development.

'Last year (1996) I ran about three Grand Prix distances for Williams and we tend to keep to a routine when I do a day's running in the car. Firstly, we generally adjust the car to my personal set-up and work from there on the programme, although in 1997 it was slightly different because I was concentrating on the new development car, with grooved tyres, in preparation for a change of rules next season.

'This called for a lot of disciplined driving. Inside, I may want to go for a fastest time, but the fact remains that I am employed to work through whatever programmes the team requires from me. You just do the job as best you can, trying not to risk damaging the car.'

Throughout the year the test team evaluates modifications and technical developments which could be transferred to the race cars during the season. In addition, it generates new ideas which might or might not see the light of competitive day on future race cars.

Meanwhile, Williams is one of the key teams contracted to carry out tyre development work for Goodyear and this also takes up a considerable amount of time.

# Chapter 3

# Engines
# and tyres

During the time in which Frank Williams has owned a Grand Prix team, engine and tyre technology has developed out of all recognition. When Piers Courage first took to the tracks in 1969 with the Williams Brabham BT26A, the ubiquitous Ford-financed Cosworth DFV was

*Fighting against the odds. Mansell with the Judd-engined Williams FW12 in the 1988 Brazilian Grand Prix.* (Formula One Pictures)

just getting into its stride as the first freely available, potentially competitive 'customer' engine of the post-war motor racing era.

The Dunlop tyres on which the car raced were grooved; the advent of F1 slicks was still two seasons away. When Frank acquired the ex-works

*Inside Renault Sport's headquarters at Viry-Chatillon, near Paris.* (Renault)

Brabham via a roundabout route from amateur racer Charles Bridges, he paid engineer Robin Herd – later one of the founders of the March company – to adapt the chassis to take the new engine. It had originally been designed round the Australian Repco V8.

In those days, of course, F1 designs were usually finalised by small groups of engineers working almost on instinct. Wind tunnel testing was virtually unknown and although Lotus

*Detailed preparation of Renault's V10s left nothing to chance, enabling the French engine maker to develop a matchless reputation for reliability.* (Renault)

chief Colin Chapman was pushing back the boundaries of F1 technology, most Grand Prix engineering work tended to centre on chassis development. Engines were very much off-the-peg accessories unless, of course, you were Ferrari and BRM who made the entire chassis/power unit package usually, it has to be said, to their comparative overall detriment.

Integrating chassis and engine design concepts became a major factor in the mid-1980s when turbocharged F1 engines became de rigeur.

---

## After three seasons in the sun the team had a cold douse of reality

---

Williams had pursued its own discreet engine development programme on the Cosworth DFV ever since 1979, using the services of John Judd's Rugby-based Engine Developments organisation as well as outside consultant Chris Walters. Much of the work concentrated on the rather fragile valvegear and, between 1979 and 1982, these Williams developments boosted the V8's output from around 480 to 540bhp. It was impressive stuff, but not sufficient to get a sniff of the new generation of 1.5-litre turbos.

As recounted, the first Honda V10 demonstrated explosively sudden power delivery; it had huge capacity, but was initially endowed with a wickedly sudden power curve which kept the drivers on their toes as the rear wheels broke traction, prompting the urgent need for great armfuls of opposite lock.

Developing an atmosphere of mutual trust with Honda was as important as integrating their iron-block V10 into a decent chassis design. Gradually Williams managed to get the message over to the Honda engine design group that a more useable power curve, better structural rigidity from the cylinder block and enhanced mechanical reliability were just as important as a good chassis.

In 1985, Patrick Head made the move to carbon-fibre composite monocoque construction which offered a more rigid chassis structure. Simultaneously Honda worked hard on engine development, their close relationship with Williams enhanced by the establishment of an in-house engine development facility at the team's Didcot factory. By the end of the season the engines were running in qualifying trim with around 1100bhp on tap, even racing on occasion with 900bhp.

Yet massaging the relationship between engine and chassis design is not the work of a moment. Historically, those partnerships which have endured the longest also turn out to be among the best. Teams which chop and change around have difficulty in establishing a decent perfor-

*Ready to go. Renault V10 installed in a Williams FW16B, 1994 Portuguese Grand Prix. Michael Schumacher, whose Benetton would be powered by a Renault the following season, doesn't seem overly impressed. (DPPI)*

# Honda, the inscrutable partners

The first Williams-Hondas were ready for their F1 debut in the final race of 1983, the South African Grand Prix at Kyalami. It was the start of a difficult development period during which the outspoken Keke Rosberg continually complained that the new car's chassis was flexing, causing handling problems. These assertions understandably annoyed Patrick Head, who understood there was a problem which the team eventually traced to a flexing cylinder block and engine mounts rather than the chassis itself.

Working smoothly with Honda meant coming to terms with the Japanese business culture and, although Keke scored the partnership's first win in the 1984 Dallas Grand Prix, it took some time for the new alliance to gell. This was not helped by a succession of spectacular piston failures during the second half of that same season which left the Williams directors grinding their teeth in frustration and privately wondering what on earth they had got themselves into.

However, a climate of mutual trust was eventually established between the two parties, and the results spoke for themselves.

*Nigel Mansell heads for victory in the 1987 British Grand Prix in the Honda-powered FW11B.* (Formula One Pictures)

*Renault Sport's chief engineer Bernard Dudot collaborates with a colleague working on a CAD/CAM screen at Viry-Chatillon.* (Renault)

mance baseline, as McLaren found between 1993 and 1995 when they used three different engines – Ford, Peugeot and Mercedes-Benz – across three separate seasons.

By 1986, even allowing for Honda's concern over Frank Williams's incapacity, the Williams-Hondas partnership was the class act of the field. The team was by now well accustomed to every nut and bolt on the Japanese V10s and remained the dominant F1 force through to the end of 1987, their final season together.

But if Williams had enjoyed three seasons in the Grand Prix sun, now came an unwelcome douse of cold reality. For 1988 the team, through force of circumstance, opted for the new 3.5-

litre naturally aspirated Judd V8 engine and equipped the new FW12 chassis with the team's own reactive suspension design which Piquet had used on the FW11B turbo to win the previous year's Italian Grand Prix at Monza.

During this interim season in which the turbos were phased out, naturally aspirated cars would be permitted to run 40kg lighter than their opposition. But having decided to rely on the reactive suspension system, Head pared the car's specification to the bone in order to make the weight limit, retaining no provision for conventional steel springing.

This proved to be a mistake. The Judd-engined Williams was beset by overheating and excessive vibration which scrambled the car's electrical system and contributed to suspension breakages. Mid-season, after first practice for the British Grand Prix at Silverstone, in fact, Head decided to make a breathtaking overnight change to conventional springing at the front of the car, the rear-end having already been altered.

This was one of those episodes which exemplifies just why Grand Prix motor racing is such a special business. At 2.30pm on Friday Head punched the 'go' button on this project. Disc springs suitable for the purpose were located in Worcester and collected by

Williams later that evening. Modified front suspension struts were provided to accept the new components, and by the small hours of Saturday morning the revised struts were being run up on the damper test-rig at Didcot.

Head arrived with the new struts at around 8.00am to find the spare car stripped ready to take the components. Both Nigel Mansell and team-mate Riccardo Patrese could scarcely believe how much better the new set-up was; Nigel used it for the race and drove to a storming second place finish, justifying the expenditure of all that midnight oil.

Long before the end of the 1988

*Comparative power. Honda's splendid twin-turbo 1.5-litre V6 installed in a 1987 Williams FW11B. (Formula One Pictures)*

season it was clear that Williams would need to rekindle a partnership with a major motor manufacturer if it was to revive its competitive edge into the new era of 3.5-litre naturally aspirated engines. The Judd V8 had been a mistake forced on the team by circumstance. Now it was time to rebuild.

In fact, barely a month after Honda and Williams had made public their intention to part company, Frank and Patrick had a preliminary meeting with Renault Sport personnel over the weekend of the 1987 Portuguese Grand Prix at Estoril. The French company had pioneered F1 turbo technology ten years earlier, but had been out of the Grand Prix arena ever since the end of 1986 when Team Lotus opted to discard its engines in favour of Honda power for the following season.

Despite this, Renault never ignored the value of Grand Prix racing as a technical and promotional tool. To that end, Renault Sport's chief engineer Bernard Dudot and a small group of engineers stayed on at the company's Viry-Chatillon headquarters working away on a 3.5-litre V10 designed for the new F1 regulations. There was, of course, no question of Renault reviving its own F1 team, which had dwindled away at the end of 1985, but the company was receptive to any ideas of

*The Judd V8 which Williams used as a stop-gap power unit in 1988 after the split with Honda. (Formula One Pictures)*

a partnership with an existing constructor, particularly one with the high profile reputation enjoyed by Williams.

A deal was duly finalised in June 1988 and the first Williams RS01 V10 engine raced at the following year's Brazilian Grand Prix installed in the Williams FW12C chassis – developments of the old Judd-engined chassis – driven by Thierry Boutsen and Riccardo Patrese.

---

## A new technical structure was used to produce the 1991 car

---

From the outset, the main problem was that the new Renault engine had not been developed for installation in a specific chassis as Dudot's team had been working on the new project for some 14 months before reaching the new agreement with Williams. This situation was duly rectified for the 1990 season when the new FW13 chassis, introduced at the end of the previous year, was powered by a heavily revised version of the Renault V10 dubbed RS2.

This not only produced more power, but was also modified to sit lower in the chassis, much to the benefit of the car's handling. Even so, the package was still not fully capable of challenging the McLaren domination of F1, so Patrick Head and his team set about developing a totally new technical structure to produce the 1991 car.

Combined with the move to invite Nigel Mansell back into the fold as team leader, Williams now took a path which would lead to World Championship domination.

In the summer of 1990, Patrick also expanded the Williams engineering team by recruiting former Leyton House F1 engineer Adrian Newey as chief designer. Up to this point, Williams had been testing an undercut nose configuration in the wind tunnel, but as they had not yet managed to finalise a front wing to match, this new development did not produce a significant performance enhancement.

However, Adrian had already experimented with a raised nose on the Leyton House CG891 design and had amassed a lot of experience with such developments. His input convinced Patrick that the new Williams FW14 should feature a high nose configuration.

Newey also produced some other novel areas of aerodynamic development, resulting in the first truly integrated Williams-Renault chassis design. Meanwhile, Renault's progress with the RS3 V10 engine in conjunction with Elf fuel technology was nothing less than sensational. It gave Honda a real fright as the Japanese company wrestled with its new V12 development programme for McLaren,

Right *The Renault V10 powered Williams to 73 Grand Prix wins between 1989 and 1997.* (both Formula One Pictures)

Overleaf *Nelson Piquet's FW11B makes a routine tyre stop en route to victory in the 1987 Italian Grand Prix.* (Formula One Pictures)

*Damon Hill with the Williams FW18 during tyre testing at Estoril, February 1996. Goodyear's long partnership with Williams produced enormous technical benefits and financial support.* (Formula One Pictures)

and Williams sustained its challenge for the World Championship pretty well through to the end of the season.

It was the start of a great era in Williams history, with Renault power propelling its cars to a glittering series of Drivers' and Constructors' World Championship titles.

# Chapter 4

# Where the money comes from

There are few professional sports as secretive about their finances as Grand Prix motor racing, so putting an accurate finger on a top F1 team's income and expenditure is necessarily a rather hit-or-miss challenge.

Nevertheless, the best evidence is that the Rothmans Williams Renault team probably spent in the region of £25 million on its 1997 World Championship-winning programme. This represents one of the biggest budgets in the business and reflects the enormous financial commitment involved in sustaining a position at the sharp end of this intensely competitive world.

The income of today's Grand Prix team comes primarily from major international corporations eager for a share of the sport's global television coverage. Across the 17 race series, if one takes into account live race broadcasts, additional feature programmes and news coverage, the FIA Formula 1 World Championship reaches around 450 million people per race worldwide.

With more than 201 countries screening over 36,000 individual broadcasts across the season, it is clear that Rothmans, for example, is getting cheap coverage for its annual investment, particularly when one takes into account the increasing restrictions on tobacco advertising in various parts of the world, most notably the European Union.

In addition, up to the end of the 1997 season Williams enjoyed the benefit of free engines from its technical partner Renault Sport. With a notional value of £200,000 each, excluding development costs, and around 30 engines being rotated through the system during the course of the year, this amounts to a benefit of

Overleaf *Dripping with sponsorship. Alain Prost's overalls in 1993 bore testimony to the enormous budgets required in F1.* (Formula One Pictures)

# How Williams got the Saudis on board

A crucial financial breakthrough came at the 1977 British Grand Prix when the Williams March began carrying sponsorship identification from Saudia, the airline of the Kingdom of Saudi Arabia.

'A guy I knew called Tony Harris worked in the London advertising agency which handled the Saudia account,' said Frank, 'and he agreed to introduce me to Mohammed Al Fawzan, the airline's sales manager in Jeddah. He arranged for our company to have a very small sponsorship deal on the rear wing of the March.'

This was a crucial foot in a commercial door. The Saudia link could be used as a calling card for Frank to use in his approaches to other Saudi Arabian companies and through connections established by Charlie Crichton-Stuart – another old mate from the F3 days in the mid-1960s – he managed to get an audience with a member of the Saudi royal family in January 1978.

Frank's audience with Prince Muhammed bin Fahd, the second eldest son of King Fahd, led to backing from Albilad, the trading company of the Saudi royal family. Then came backing from the Ojjeh family's TAG group, today a partner in the West McLaren Mercedes team, which helped the Williams team finance its crucial expansion and rise to competitiveness between 1979 and 1983.

*Backing from the high tech TAG group was one of the benefits yielded from the Saudi connections in the early 1980s.* (Formula One Pictures)

around £6 million plus the same again in terms of a contribution to the team's budget.

Income from technical sponsors such as Castrol, for lubricants, and tyre suppliers Goodyear are estimated in the region of £3 million, plus technical back-up and free products. In the case of tyres alone, this could include as much as £250,000 a year in pure unit

*Title sponsorship of the team also gains identification on the team's huge transporters.*
(Formula One Pictures)

costs, disregarding the enormous sums staked by the tyre companies in terms of research and development.

In 1997, other technical partners included Komatsu (gear technology), Automotive Products (brakes and clutch), Magneti Marelli (electronics) and Champion (sparking plugs).

There is a raft of additional sponsors include Sonax car care products, Henderson Investors, Andersen Consulting – who masterminded the team's complex move from Didcot to Grove as part of their sponsorship package – plus Falke textiles and the German digital television channel

DF1. Then there are many official suppliers from the motor racing industry such as OZ wheels, Digital, Sparco, Telxon, Largotim, Burg-Wachter and Snap-on Tools. A conservative estimate suggests these amount to a minimum of £7 million in total.

## Tobacco money has kept F1 on track for the past 30 years

The business of negotiating the details of such diverse sponsors and investors is obviously a full-time job. Senior acquisitions manager Jim Wright heads a department of nine people who administer and service their requirements, helping sponsoring companies to maximise their association with the team.

Charting television income is more difficult, but sources suggest that Williams should have been due around £12 million as its share from TV income in 1997. In addition, there are even less specific payments from race income which depends on a complex formula based on historical results, qualifying positions and the Constructors' Championship points achieved during the immediately previous two half seasons.

However, a possible income of around £50 million has to be set against an outlay of at least £5 million annually on the initial development of the next season's car, plus around £3 million actually building, say, six new chassis to that specification, and now of course the £13 million annual engine fee to Mecachrome.

Research and development, in order to sustain the team's competitive edge in years to come, could swallow up £6 million, while the company's annual running costs including salaries for the 400-plus workforce are likely to be in the order of £18 million. Set alongside those figures, the driver retainers for Jacques Villeneuve (£6 million) and Heinz-Harald Frentzen (£2 million) look like mere footnotes on the balance sheet.

The 1998 and 1999 F1 seasons will see Williams continuing its partnership with Rothmans International, although the distinctive blue and white livery carried by the team's cars since the start of 1994 will be swept away and replaced with the red identification of Winfield, another of the Rothmans International brands.

Winfield is Australia's top-selling cigarette brand which is also available in South Africa, New Zealand, Malaysia and France. Plans for the near future also include an expansion of a target market in Europe, including the Netherlands and Luxembourg. Clearly, despite the controversial aspects of tobacco sponsorship, Rothmans feel that, for the immediate future at least, a high profile involvement with Grand Prix motor racing through the Williams squad is both profitable and appropriate.

*In 1984, Keke Rosberg had personal sponsorship from ICI in addition to the company's backing of the team as a whole.* (Formula One Pictures)

There are, of course, powerful emotional issues at stake here. Flick through the F1 history books and you will see plenty of Grand Prix drivers puffing at cigarettes during the 1950s and 1960s, but as the sport became more physically demanding through the 1970s, the image of an F1 driver tossing aside his stogie before hopping into the cockpit became progressively thinner on the ground.

With today's generation of Grand Prix drivers existing on a diet frequently no more adventurous than pasta, salads and apple juice, the idea of Jacques Villeneuve or Heinz-Harald Frentzen lighting up a Winfield on the starting grid is as likely as their casting aside their helmet in favour of a leather flying cap. Yet the fact remains that as long as cigarettes are legally available products, the tobacco companies will milk the potential of a global sport such as F1 for all it is worth. Williams officially remains coy and uncommunicative on the question of this contradiction. Understandably so, one might add.

In truth, of course, tobacco companies have permitted Grand Prix teams to keep on track for the last 30 years. It was Colin Chapman who introduced the Players' Gold Leaf brand to F1 on the works Lotus cars in 1968 – three years after cigarette advertising was banned on British television – and since then

*Thierry Boutsen with former Williams commercial director Sheridan Thynne (left) and future Williams driver Ayrton Senna, then driving for McLaren, during a 1990 test session at Silverstone.* (Formula One Pictures)

*The Brazilian Banco Nacional was one of Ayrton Senna's personal sponsors throughout his racing career.* (Formula One Pictures)

the tobacco companies' influence has expanded to a position of near-dominance. In 1997, every front-running Grand Prix team had a major cigarette maker in its portfolio of sponsors.

However, things could change for teams such as Williams in the future. Bernie Ecclestone's F1 Holdings empire was, as of December 1997, poised for a Stock Exchange flotation

# Far Eastern promise if tobacco is banned?

By remaining publicly silent on the issue, Williams and other top F1 teams have tacitly endorsed the line adopted by FIA president Max Mosley late in 1997 when he made it clear to the British and other EU governments that there was a chance of Grand Prix racing effectively decamping to the Pacific Rim unless planned restrictions on tobacco advertising were eased.

This has become a highly sensitive political issue. Tony Blair's New Labour administration demonstrated hesitancy and inexperience in trying to field the persuasive arguments from the highly influential F1 lobby. Williams and the other British-based teams must have breathed a sigh of relief when Blair signalled that his government would offer an open-ended exemption to F1, a strategy which seemed certain to scupper an EU-wide ban on tobacco promotions in all sports.

However, when subjected to intense pressure from other EU governments, the British politicians began talking in terms of a nine year period of grace in which F1 could find other non-tobacco sponsors. It now remains to be seen whether motor racing's governing body can sanction a sufficiently large number of races in South East Asia in order to put some weight behind its threat to progressively withdraw from Europe unless that open-ended tobacco advertising exemption is reinstated.

With many Asian economies suffering badly at the time of writing, the FIA's notion that teams such as Williams would actually move their headquarters to the Pacific Rim can confidently be dismissed as impractical pie-in-the-sky muscle flexing. Grand Prix racing will remain essentially a European-based sport with jobs, factories and technology staying where they are for the present.

which could put a value of around £1.6 billion effectively on the future of F1 as a promotional corporate tool. Ecclestone is convinced that the advent of digital pay-to-view television channels will boost F1's income to the point where the sport could effectively be self-financing from television income alone. This, in turn, could mean more sponsors on each individual car, with the underlying implication that the more companies who do come in, the less influence each could wield over the various teams' fortunes.

This is all theoretical stuff, of course, and there is no doubt that the tobacco companies will continue to wield considerable financial clout for the foreseeable future. Interestingly, however, the Williams contract with Winfield lasts only until the end of 1999, the eve of BMW's re-entry into the sport as the team's engine partner from the start of the 2000 season. F1 observers will be interested to see whether BMW's inclination might be to steer its new Grand Prix partner away from tobacco sponsorship, or simply acquiesce with the current state of the business.

# Chapter 5

# The men
# at the wheel

It was the two second places achieved by Piers Courage in the 1969 Monaco and US Grands Prix which cemented Frank Williams's reputation as a Formula 1 entrant. True

*The golden partnership: Frank Williams and Piers Courage.*

there would be distinctly rocky times ahead, but this season with the smart dark blue Brabham-Ford both provided the bedrock on which Frank's subsequent achievements were built – and proved that it was still possible for a well-drilled private team to embarrass the works runners.

Although those two second places represented the peak of Piers's achievement, his run in the leading bunch at Monza before his car developed fuel starvation problems was regarded by some as an even more significant index of his progress.

'To my mind that was the day Piers came of age as a Grand Prix driver,' remembers Jackie Stewart. 'Up until that point, I had always been just a little concerned about his unpredictability in close traffic, but he ran with the leading bunch – Jochen Rindt, Jean-Pierre Beltoise and me – for many laps and I never had a moment's worry. He was driving immaculately and with total discipline.'

After Courage's death, Williams struggled through what was left of his de Tomaso partnership first with Brian Redman, then former Brabham driver Tim Schenken. But for the 1971 season he started with a clean sheet of paper when he purchased a new March 711 and signed Frenchman Henri Pescarolo to drive it. The son of one of France's leading surgeons, Pescarolo had himself been a medical student until motor racing got in the way and he was carried along on the flood tide of France's 1960s motor racing revival along with Beltoise and the Matra company.

After winning the 1967 European F3 Championships, 'Pesca' moved into F2, but his career plans were almost ruined when he sustained severe facial burns while testing a Matra sports car at Le Mans in the spring of 1969. In 1970 he was promoted to the works Matra F1 team, but dropped in favour of New Zealander Chris Amon at the end of the year.

The bearded Frenchman spent two years driving for Williams, but never achieved much in the way of worthwhile results. 'You must remember that in those days I was starry-eyed, full of enthusiasm for whatever I turned my hand to,' recalls Frank. 'I had believed in Piers, so I believed in the next one, if you like. Pesca had been good in F2, extremely brave in the Matra at Le Mans, not lifting off at night in the rain, and so-on, so I was full of enthusiasm for him. But he wasn't quite top F1 material and we never quite gelled. We were always struggling.'

In 1972 Williams also gave an F1 break to Carlos Pace, the promising young Brazilian driver, and in 1973 relied on the services of the taciturn Kiwi Howden Ganley. The ever-popular Arturo Merzario drove for Williams in 1974, the skinny Italian partnered by effervescent Jacques Laffite who would become a great Williams favourite and was asked back into the team many years later for the 1983 and 1984 seasons as Keke Rosberg's team-mate.

## The team had progressed from sad also-rans to potential winners

Frank subsequently admitted that it had probably been a mistake having Laffite back for a second stint, but the team loved the irreverent Frenchman with whom it was virtually impossible to get annoyed. 'There wasn't really anybody else available on the market of appropriate status, and you have to remember that Jacques had then won six Grands Prix. But he was never quicker than the car. While Keke could lift a car to a level beyond its immediate potential, selecting Jacques was perhaps an error of judgement, with hindsight.'

Sheridan Thynne recalls one episode which captures Laffite's enchanting character. At Spa prior to the 1983 Belgian Grand Prix, the Frenchman was late for a pre-race briefing. Frank and his colleagues were getting impatient and the team boss, having looked out of the window and seen Jacques sauntering casually across the paddock, announced 'I'm going to give him a bollocking.'

'Jacques breezed in,' he remembered, 'and said "allo everybody. This week I watched old films on the video to improve my English, so what's new pussycat?" And with that he gave Frank a kiss on the cheek. Everybody dissolved into laughter. Jacques later admitted he realised he would have to do something to defuse the situation. Which he did.'

Between Laffite's two stints driving for Frank the team had progressed from being pathetic also-rans to consistent potential winners. And the man who had the biggest impact in that respect was Alan Jones.

Throughout the mid-1970s, there must have been many occasions when the only member of the international motor racing fraternity who believed he was World Championship material was Jones himself. Born in Melbourne on 2 November 1946, Alan had grown up in a world of cars and motor racing. His father was the larger-than-life Aussie driver Stan Jones who raced Maseratis and Coopers throughout the 1950s and, despite falling on hard times and encountering ill-health, became one of his son's greatest fans when the time came for Alan to try making his own mark in the sport.

Stan Jones was a tough nut. The fact that he had been debilitated by a stroke in no way softened his fiery

*Mansell's 1987 title hopes ended with this crash in practice for the Japanese Grand Prix at Suzuka.* (Formula One Pictures)

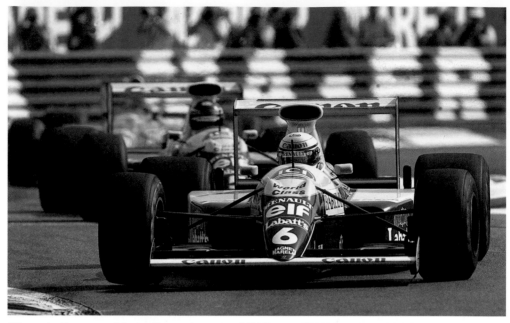

*Riccardo Patrese with the Renault-engined Williams FW12C in the 1989 German Grand Prix.* (Formula One Pictures)

personality. During the 1970 Brazilian Torneio Formula 3 series, Jones senior chased the Lotus team manager Peter Warr out of his son's pit, brandishing one of his crutches, after Warr had raised a query over the legality of Alan's private Brabham. Jones junior inherited the same feisty character.

Alan only just missed out on winning the 1973 British F3 Championship and eventually got his F1 break in 1975 driving a private Hesketh-Ford. From there he moved into Graham Hill's Embassy F1 squad for part of 1975, thence to Team Surtees the following year where he raised a few eyebrows by leading the non-title Race of Champions at Brands Hatch ahead of James Hunt, the man who would go on to become the 1976 World Champion.

Jones may not have appeared to be a natural ace, but he was clearly endowed with enormous strength and determination. He fell out with Surtees by the end of 1976 and looked set to languish in some US domestic racing backwater, but his F1 chances were revived in the wake of Tom Pryce's tragic fatal accident in the 1977 South African Grand Prix. Casting round for a replacement, the Shadow team decided to give Jones a chance. He drove well for the balance of the season, and when Hunt's McLaren suffered engine failure in the Austrian Grand Prix, Alan was on hand to post the first F1 victory of his career.

By the end of that season Jones had done enough to get himself noticed. His emergence as a decent F1 driver coincided with Williams's rebirth as a team. For 1978 they were looking for a new driver to grow with them. As

Frank admits, he and Patrick had whittled down to a short list comprising Hans-Joachim Stuck, Gunnar Nilsson and Jones:

'By the time we were ready to make our choice, I suppose you could say that Jonesey became ours by the defection of the others. If you work backwards over the years, you can see that we've made all sorts of bum driver selections, but Jones was a great one.

'That said, it certainly wasn't premeditated in the sense that we recognised him as a great talent. We thought he would be nice and steady, get us some points and keep us in the Constructors' Association.'

Jones knew what he wanted. He asked Williams for a £40,000 retainer in 1978, but, more importantly, he had correctly discerned the team's potential. He judged that Frank's team was going places and he wanted to be part of that action. As early as the second race of the season, he laid down a marker as to what might be coming by qualifying the taut new Williams FW06 on the fourth row of the grid at Rio de Janeiro.

In the history of every Grand Prix team, there is a turning point, a crucial moment which rings a bell and signals 'these people are worth watching.' For Williams, this day came at Long Beach, California, on the occasion of the 1978 United States Grand Prix West. Many people recall this event as the first to be led by Gilles Villeneuve at the wheel of a Ferrari; yet when Gilles retired from the fray after tripping over Clay Regazzoni's tail-end Shadow, it was Jones who grabbed the headlines for Williams.

From eighth position on the start-

*Patrese in the Williams FW13B in the 1990 Italian Grand Prix.* (Formula One Pictures)

ing grid, Alan stormed through to hold third place behind Villeneuve and his Maranello team-mate Carlos Reutemann. After Gilles's unceremonious departure, Jones ran second from lap 39 to 62, hardly slowing his pace as the FW06's full-width nose wing progressively collapsed to drag its outer extremities along the surface of the track.

## When you are starving you'll eat rabbit food if necessary

The final phase of the race was an anti-climax. Jones faded to seventh with fuel pick-up problems. But by then Frank Williams was grinning like a Cheshire cat.

'I never dreamt we would be capable of running that high,' he said. 'It utterly convinced me that we had signed the right man.' In fact, mid-way through the race, Williams had turned to Charlie Crichton-Stuart on the pit wall and said, 'I really don't care now if he fails to finish this race – he's the most exciting driver I've seen since Ronnie Peterson.'

The partnership took off. By the end of the season the FW06 was acknowledged as a pretty effective racing car, even though a couple of stub-axle failures caused the car to fly off the road. Luckily Jones wasn't hurt in either incident, but he didn't stint when it came to glowering with displeasure at Patrick Head over the incidents. For his part, Patrick admits that working with Jones really focused his mind for the first time on the possibility that Grand Prix racing would provide him with a full-time career:

'I suppose I came through the transitional phase from thinking that it was all really a bit of fun, and maybe I'll do something else next year, to realising that this was all really quite good and, if we put our noses out, then we might seriously be able to achieve something.

'From then on, I began to take things more seriously, and the hub shaft failure at Watkins Glen in practice was really quite a sobering experience. We'd had something similar at Zandvoort where Alan went off during practice for the Dutch Grand Prix, but I don't think I'd quite analysed what happened in sufficient detail, nor taken sufficient steps to make certain it didn't happen again.'

In 1979 Williams expanded to a two car team with the affable Swiss Clay Regazzoni lining up alongside Jones. 'Clay was similar to Laffite,' said Frank. 'An easy-going guy, but he wasn't quite quick enough in qualifying, so he was obviously shown up by Alan.'

Ironically, it was Regazzoni who posted the team's first F1 victory in the 1979 British Grand Prix at Silverstone. Jones had retired in the lead with water pump failure. But it was Alan who then clicked onto a winning streak, triumphing in the German, Austrian, Dutch and Canadian Grands Prix to wind up third in the World Championship.

Williams had now changed into a higher gear. The team was fully competitive and an obvious title chal-

# Mansell and Piquet, the unlikely partnership

It took only a few races in 1986 for Nelson Piquet to get irritated by the fact that his Williams team-mate Nigel Mansell was beating him so frequently. He firmly believed that he'd been guaranteed unconditional number one status in the team and that meant Mansell should play second fiddle. This state of affairs would eventually cause a breach between Piquet and the team by the end of 1987.

'What Nelson thought he was being guaranteed was a repeat of the Reutemann fiasco of 1981 when we controlled – or tried to control – the second driver,' said Frank much later. 'What in fact had been discussed was that, in a classic case of one driver leading the Championship and needing every bit of support, then we would control his team-mate.

'But he was not given unconditional priority over the second driver. We took the view that if they were both running for the Championship they would have to fight it out between them.'

It was quite a difficult situation. Mansell, highly motivated and aggressive, felt challenged by the flip side of the equation. As far as he was concerned, all bets were off. He would race Piquet tooth and nail, privately believing that he could undermine the Brazilian's confidence with his blistering speed. If Nelson was the more tactical driver, then Nigel certainly proved that he was generally the quicker.

*Team-mates. Nigel Mansell (in car) and Nelson Piquet dominated F1 for Frank's team in 1986/7, but their rivalry indirectly ripped asunder the Williams-Honda alliance.* (Formula One Pictures)

lenger. With that in mind, Frank and Patrick decided it was necessary to strengthen the driver line-up for 1980. Regazzoni's contract was not renewed, his place being taken by the rather taciturn, moody, but undeniably brilliant Carlos Reutemann.

## Very clever people do not fight battles they will lose

The Argentine driver had previously won races for Brabham and Ferrari, but squandered the 1979 season with an ill-judged, if understandable, move to Lotus. Approaching his 38th birthday, he knew he had to get back behind the wheel of a competitive car if his F1 career wasn't to peter out altogether. He signed as number two to Jones. 'When you are a starving man, you eat rabbit food, if necessary,' he later remarked. 'You are thankful for anything you can get.'

Reutemann returned to the winner's circle with victory in the 1980 Monaco Grand Prix, but this season truly belonged to Jones. Confident wins in Argentina, France, Britain, Canada and the USA yielded the World Championship. For Frank, it could be regarded as Mission Accomplished.

Reutemann later admitted he had experienced some difficulties getting to grips with the challenge of 1980. 'The first year with Frank was tough from a driving point of view. I was completely out of shape. At the end of 1978 I changed from Ferrari to Lotus, but although the Lotus 79 had been competitive the previous year, it was certainly not good in 1979. As a result, I had no real experience of a ground effect car until 1980 and it took me quite a time to develop the best driving technique to deal with them.'

Even in 1981, Carlos would find himself hamstrung by the need to defer to Jones in certain situations. His Williams contract contained what was known as the 'seven second' clause. In a nutshell, if he found himself running more than seven seconds ahead of the Australian, then he could win the race. If Jones was less than seven seconds behind, in second place, of course, then Carlos had to let him past.

In the 1981 Brazilian Grand Prix at Rio, it was more than Carlos could stomach. He led from the start on a wet track, with Jones dutifully falling in behind him. Alan clearly believed that Reutemann would do his duty, but the driver from Argentina just couldn't bring himself to relinquish his advantage. Jones duly finished second and was furious. 'With good reason,' added Reutemann.

The Williams team never paid Reutemann any money at all for that win. Shrewdly, he never queried the lack of payment. 'That was an indication of how exceptionally clever he was,' noted Sheridan Thynne. 'Very clever people never fight battles they are going to lose.'

Jones should have retained his

*Boutsen with the FW13B in the 1990 Spanish Grand Prix.* (Formula One Pictures)

World Championship in 1981. The revised Williams FW07C was still pretty competitive, but some bad luck and unexpected mechanical glitches cost him victory at Monaco and Hockenheim. It was enough to lose him a clear shot at the title. Reutemann went into the final race at Las Vegas on pole position, yet had inexplicably faded to eighth at the chequered flag. As a result, Nelson Piquet won the Championship for Brabham.

## The Rolex, the gold bracelet, the Gucci case – he's very fast!

By then, Jones had decided to retire at the end of the season. That left Reutemann as de facto team leader and, after some fleeting contact with Niki Lauda who eventually made an F1 comeback with rivals McLaren, Frank and Patrick eventually opted to gamble on signing the extrovert Finn Keke Rosberg.

Rosberg had wrestled his way to F1 prominence via a bumpy route through Super Vee, F2 and Formula Atlantic before finally getting into F1 with the Theodore team in 1978. That year he put his name up in lights by winning the rain-soaked Silverstone International Trophy race.

In 1980 and 1981 he drove for the Fittipaldi F1 team whose star was by now fading dramatically. He won the Williams drive after testing against Frenchman Jean-Pierre Jarier. He was brash, extrovert and a chain smoker. Reutemann noted with gentle irony, 'I tell you Frank: long blond hair, the Rolex, the gold identity bracelet, the Gucci briefcase . . . I think he is very quick, Frank!'

Rosberg was just that. Yet by the same token, he could be painfully outspoken. Frank recalls, 'during his first season in particular, in terms of communication with the team's engineers, he was given to making erratic, nonsensical and sweeping statements.' But the relationship matured quickly after Keke won the 1982 World Championship, the last to be won by a Cosworth V8-engined car in the pre-turbo era.

Reutemann had decided to quit after only two races in 1982. Following the Brazilian Grand Prix and his crash with Arnoux, he knew he'd lost the spark. By his own admission, he was driving badly, didn't care about anything and was starting to make mistakes. It was a shame, for the dignified, highly principled Argentine driver was a man of enormous talent and honour, one of a handful of genuine stars in F1 history who didn't win the Championship, but certainly deserved to achieve that distinction.

His departure meant that the burden of team leadership fell on Rosberg's shoulders. He would be partnered by the popular Irishman Derek Daly for the balance of that season, then by

*Nigel Mansell at Didcot prior to the 1992 pre-season press conference for what turned out to be his World Championship year. (Formula One Pictures)*

*Monaco was one of the few races which did not go Mansell's way in 1992; he had to be content with being second to Senna.* (Formula One Pictures)

Laffite in 1983 and 1984 and finally by Nigel Mansell in 1985. During his Williams career, despite complaining that the team 'never forgave me for not being Alan Jones,' Rosberg won five Grands Prix. Most observers believe he had the talent to have won many more.

Keke spent his final year in F1 partnering Alain Prost at McLaren in 1986. But he felt a great affection for Frank Williams's team: 'I had a tremendous time there and will always be very grateful for the break they gave me. They were a very special bunch of people. I still feel more at home with Williams than I ever did with McLaren, because that was Alain's team and I never quite integrated with them in the same way.'

Then came the big break. In the summer of 1985, Frank Williams forged a deal with twice World Champion Nelson Piquet to lead his team the following year. Mansell was already in situ after a four year stint at Lotus during which he had won not a single race. Williams's view was that he would be a good steady number two, but the moustachioed man from Birmingham soon proved that he was very much better than that.

Piquet's arrival also coincided with the introduction of the Williams-Honda FW11. The Anglo-Japanese technical partnership had really gelled by the start of 1986 and Piquet opened the season with a great win in Brazil. Mansell went off on the second lap after a skirmish with Ayrton Senna's Lotus, but if Nelson allowed himself a quiet giggle at his team-mate's fate, that would quickly be wiped from his face as Nigel got into top gear as the season progressed.

# Damon Hill, a fair deal or not?

Damon Hill had learnt his front-line F1 trade as Prost's team-mate in 1993, winning a hat-trick of Grands Prix during the second half of the season. He was clearly an accomplished driver whose technical feed-back was improving all the time.

Yet somehow, having come up from the test driving role, he would always be perceived by some of the Williams hierachy as the tea boy who'd been given the keys to the executive dining room. He was a home-brewed Williams product, not bought in from the outside. In that respect he was somewhat undervalued.

Yet in 1994, Damon rose to the challenge. Just as his father had helped Team Lotus to regroup following the death of Jim Clark in 1968, so Damon steadied Williams morale after Senna's death. He won the Spanish, British, Italian, Portuguese and Japanese Grands Prix to get within one point of dislodging Michael Schumacher from his World Championship lead, but the title was eventually decided in the German's favour after the two men collided in the final race of the year at Adelaide. It was one of the most controversial episodes in recent F1 history which many people, to this day, believe was a deliberate foul on Schumacher's part (particularly so in view of his tactics at Jerez in 1997).

Two years later, Hill would get his own back by winning the World Championship fair and square, to universal rejoicing.

*Damon Hill started out as the team's test driver, eventually becoming the sport's only second generation World Champion in 1996.* (Formula One Pictures)

Having lost the 1986 World Championship at the final race in Adelaide, Piquet won it in 1987, then decided to jump ship. He switched to Lotus in the wake of Ayrton Senna's decision to transfer to McLaren. Nelson was highly rated and respected by Honda, so his move saved Lotus's engine supply contract. But Senna was also going to have Honda engines at McLaren. Williams found themselves left in the lurch.

Mansell remained loyal for 1988, posting a strong second place at Silverstone in the troublesome Judd-engined Williams FW12. But this would be the first season since 1979 that the team failed to win a single race. There was a Renault V10 engine contract in the pipeline for 1989, sure enough, but that didn't keep Nigel in the fold. At the end of 1988, he decided to sign a Ferrari contract for the following year.

*Damon Hill close to tears after his Williams suffered a rare engine failure in the 1993 British Grand Prix.* (Formula One Pictures)

Senna very nearly came to Williams in 1988. It would have saved the Honda deal had he done so, but in talks with Frank Williams it became clear that he too was concerned about the boss's lack of physical mobility. They would talk again in the middle of 1990, when Ayrton's initial three year deal with McLaren was approaching its expiry, but eventually he decided to stay with Ron Dennis's team.

All this left Williams running through 1989 and 1990 with the driver line-up of Thierry Boutsen and Riccardo Patrese. Both were enor-mously popular, but not quite out of the top drawer. To be fair, neither were the Williams-Renaults those two seasons.

Nevertheless, Boutsen won the 1989 Canadian and Australian Grands Prix, both brilliant victories in soaking wet conditions, and in 1990 Patrese won at Imola and Thierry again at Budapest, on that memorable occasion managing to keep his pal Ayrton Senna's much faster McLaren boxed in behind him to the chequered flag. 'If you hadn't been a friend, I might have taken you off,' Ayrton is reputed to have remarked to

him as they climbed from their cars immediately after the chase was over.

Meanwhile, Mansell had been getting what he regarded as the rough end of a Ferrari partnership with Alain Prost throughout the 1990 season. His car, he reasoned, seemed to break down more frequently than the Frenchman's. Why? Perhaps he was being stitched up, perhaps it was just bad luck. Either way, before the end of the season he decided that he would quit F1 at the end of the year.

---

## Williams-Renault had now built up an unstoppable momentum

---

Williams, however, suspected that Nigel might have made an over-emotional judgement. With Adrian Newey now aboard to complement Patrick Head on the design side, and Renault raising the stakes in terms of engine development, Frank was confident that the team's technical package would soon become extremely competitive.

Shortly before the end of the season, Sheridan Thynne's negotiations with Mansell on Williams's behalf finally bore fruit. Mansell, by now free of any on-going Ferrari commitment, reversed his retirement decision and signed for Williams for 1991.

The 1991 Williams FW14 turned out to be just the ticket. From the outset it provided Mansell with a highly competitive tool with which to battle against the still-dominant McLaren-Hondas. He won the French, British, German, Italian and Spanish Grands Prix in dominant style, carrying his bid for the Championship all the way to the penultimate race at Suzuka where Senna finally clinched the crown.

The Williams-Renault alliance had now built up an almost unstoppable momentum. Equipped with such sophisticated electronic ancillaries as traction control, active suspension and automatic gearchange, the following year's FW14B evolution enabled Mansell to blitz his way to the 1992 Championship with nine victories. Senna and McLaren were defeated and Mansell had the title crown wrapped up by the Hungarian Grand Prix in the middle of August.

But all was not contentment. Mansell had earned a reputed £4.6 million retainer in 1991 and won the 1992 title for a slightly increased £5 million. For 1993, Williams's connections with Elf and Renault steered the team towards signing Alain Prost as Riccardo Patrese's replacement. Mansell – not the most easygoing of characters – had his misgivings over this arrangement, feeling apprehensive about being partnered with Prost after his experience at Ferrari. But a fee of £937,000 was agreed as additional compensation for having to relinquish his absolute number one status. Despite fairly troubled relations between himself and the team, it looked as though a deal had been struck.

If Mansell had been able to sign the Williams offer early, all would have

*Prost clinched his fourth World Championship with second place in the 1993 Portuguese Grand Prix, but was not prepared to stay in the team to partner Senna the following year.* (Formula One Pictures)

been well. But Elf, whose profits had fallen by 23 per cent during the first six months of 1992, had second thoughts about how much they wanted to spend on F1. Williams offered Mansell a substantially lower figure. He refused.

Crunch time came at the 1992 Italian Grand Prix where Nigel convened a press conference announcing that he would leave F1 at the end of the season. A last-minute intervention by a Williams emissary, who arrived with word from Frank that a deal could be reached, came too late. Mansell was already mid-way through his statement. The partnership had now passed beyond the point of no return.

By the time Prost arrived at Williams, he had won three World Championships and was regarded as possibly the greatest driver of his era. At the end of 1991 he had been fired by the Ferrari team because of the candour with which he described his car's deficiencies. There had been a move for him to take charge of the French Ligier team as the basis for a French national F1 operation, but the whole thing fell through and Alain chose to sit out the 1992 season. Then came the Williams offer and the Frenchman was ready to go once again.

The 1993 season started precariously when the Williams entries for the Championship were lodged two days after the final date required. This sloppy piece of housekeeping briefly

*In 1994 the brilliant Ayrton Senna joined the Rothmans Williams line-up. Here he is at Interlagos where he spun off in front of his home crowd while chasing Michael Schumacher's Benetton.* (Formula One Pictures)

put the team at the mercy of its rivals, since the rules stipulated that any late entries needed the unanimous agreement of all the other signatories to the Concorde Agreement. Eventually the team was allowed back into the fold. Max Mosley, the FIA president, unilaterally overruled the reservations of the rival teams, but still imposed a ban on all sophisticated electronic control systems – round which much of the Williams FW14B's performance advantage had been based – as from the start of the 1994 season.

Prost won his fourth World Championship with Williams in 1993, but somehow one felt he was never quite the part of the team that had been hoped. It is difficult to pinpoint why. Perhaps, in his heart of hearts, Frank Williams wanted a driver who seemed less inhibited behind the wheel. Perhaps he thought Alain a little too tactical and cautious. Or perhaps he was already dreaming about signing Ayrton Senna for 1994.

Prost had vetoed Senna coming into the team for 1993, but Frank wasn't about to permit that again the following year, even if Alain did have a contract with him through to the end of 1994.

One man who could see the futility of attempting to pair Senna and Prost

*Damon Hill did his best to restore Williams morale after Senna's death with victory in the 1994 Spanish Grand Prix.* (ICN UK Bureau)

again was McLaren boss Ron Dennis. He'd run the two men in 1988 and 1989 and appreciated just what a horror show it could turn into.

'There were suggestions that Frank was trying to create a super team, to have Prost and Senna together,' he pondered. 'But I knew there was never a chance of that. In what they are seeking to achieve, they are very similar, but that's about it. Ayrton and Alain have very different attitudes towards their team-mates, for example. Alain's motor racing philosophy is a very simple one: he is there to win and it doesn't matter if it's by a second or a minute.

'That is why, in 1993, victories that could have been more spectacular – lapping the field and so on – were not there. Prost would see that as superfluous, and I think that reflected positively on Damon Hill (his team-mate) and probably helped him. He felt stronger and more motivated, and therefore was a stronger driver.

'But if you crush someone, he can't even do what he is capable of doing, and that was one of Ayrton's strategies. He destroyed his team-mates psychologically. Whoever they were, he would always work on the psychology of the process. Motor racing made up an incredibly big percentage of Ayrton's life, a much bigger percentage than with most drivers.'

Thus it came to pass that Senna would drive for Williams in 1994. He would be partnered by Damon Hill,

*Hill and David Coulthard, Williams team-mates after Senna's death.* (ICN UK Bureau)

son of the twice World Champion Graham Hill who had been killed in an air crash when Damon was a teenager. Hill had been recruited as the Williams test driver in 1991 and promoted to race driver two years later after Mansell's defection to Indycars. He was to have more of an impact on the team's history than could ever have been imagined.

## *Senna arrived determined to win his fourth world title*

Senna came to Williams determined to win a fourth World Championship. In 1993 circumstances had obliged McLaren to rely on a customer Ford HB V8 engine to power its MP4/8 challenger. This McLaren was unquestionably a terrific chassis, the engine was light and responsive, and Ayrton's motivation was beyond question. He won five races in the car, but it was still small beer matched against what McLaren had come to expect during its years of Honda-propelled domination.

In moving to Frank's operation, Senna was totally focused on the task of reviving his position at the head of the F1 field. This felt particularly urgent in view of the challenge – much trumpeted by the media – from Benetton *wunderkind* Michael Schumacher. But the 1994 Williams FW16 proved initially difficult to drive. Senna spun off chasing Schumacher in Brazil, the first race of

the season, then slid off the road at the first corner of the Pacific Grand Prix at Aida after making contact with Mika Hakkinen's McLaren. But by the time the European season began at Imola, modifications to the FW16 had improved its performance and Ayrton qualified on pole position.

'To be honest, we made a bloody awful cock-up,' reflected Adrian Newey on the Williams's early season form. 'The lack of rear-end grip was purely a set-up problem. We were learning about springs and dampers all over again after concentrating on active suspension for two years. We also had a rather silly aerodynamic problem – basically the front wing was too low – but that was raised for Imola, by which time we were looking in pretty good shape.'

Yet the 1994 San Marino Grand Prix would become the blackest race weekend for over 30 years. During Saturday qualifying, the Austrian rookie Roland Ratzenberger was killed in a high-speed accident at the wheel of his Simtek-Ford. Then on Sunday, as Ayrton led the pack into the seventh lap of the race, harried by Schumacher, his Williams ploughed into the concrete wall on the flat-out Tamburello corner. Part of the car's suspension speered through his helmet.

FIA medical supremo Professor Sid Watkins was on the scene in moments. A close personal friend of Senna, he subjugated his emotions to the urgency of the situation. From the moment he lifted the Brazilian's vizor, he could see

*Getting things clear on the pit wall.*
*(Formula One Pictures)*

that it was dire. Ayrton had sustained a major injury to his right forehead and, as the race was red-flagged to a halt, he was air-lifted to Bologna's Maggiore Hospital where he died just four hours later.

'Everybody in the company was truly shattered by what happened,' said Frank. 'They all felt a certain responsibility, and that's still on the minds of many people here. At the end of the day, the fact is that Ayrton died in a Williams car.

'I feel very embarrassed that he never got a fair crack of the whip at Williams. He wanted to come here, and he'd wanted to for some time. People close to him have since told me that Ayrton remained pretty certain he would be World Champion in 1994. With hindsight, I think he would have been. I mean, at that time Damon

*Mansell was invited back into the Williams fold for some guest outings in 1994, crowning his return with a victory in the Australian Grand Prix. Despite this, Williams opted for Coulthard rather than himself for 1995.* (Formula One Pictures)

certainly wasn't in the same league in terms of getting to a problem, analysing it and presenting it to the engineers for solution.'

In the aftermath of Senna's death, Hill inherited the mantle of team leader, and did a magnificent job of safeguarding the team's morale. Meanwhile Renault had bankrolled Mansell's return to the team on a guest driving basis, taking the wheel whenever his US commitments to the Newman Haas team permitted. After the heady experience of omnipotence on both sides of the Atlantic – the only driver to win back-to-back F1 and Indycar titles – Mansell was feeling demotivated by the uncompetitive 1994 Indycar and wanted to return to Britain and Williams full-time for 1995. But eventually Frank and Patrick opted to promote their latest test driver, the well-scrubbed and promising Scot David Coulthard to the race team alongside Damon.

For 1995 – after being pipped to the title the previous year following a controversial crash with Schumacher in the very last race – Hill started out determined to win the Championship,

# Behind the scenes at the Senna investigation

While Damon Hill was storming to his 1996 title, the judicial examination of the circumstances surrounding Senna's fatal crash was still grinding on behind the scenes. Magistrate Maurizio Passarini had been appointed to carry out a wide-ranging investigation into the accident, in conjunction with a panel of experts which included former Ferrari engineers Mauro Forghieri and Tomasso Carletti, ex-Ferrari team manager Roberto Nosetto, retired F1 driver (and successful touring car driver) Emanuele Pirro and Professor Dalamonte, an authority on sports medicine based at the University of Bologna.

Initially there was speculation around the possibility of a broken steering column being the cause of the accident. This was fuelled by photographs of the wrecked Williams showing the car's steering wheel, still attached to a section of its shaft, in the debris alongside the car.

Inevitably, the official investigation proceeded painfully slowly with Williams engineers being permitted only the most cursory examination of the wrecked car. Not until December 1996 was it announced that Frank Williams, Patrick Head, Adrian Newey, race director Roland Bruynseraede and Imola officials Giorgio Poggi and Federico Bendenelli would be charged with culpable homicide, effectively involuntary manslaughter.

The ramifications were horrifying. FIA president Max Mosley warned that the decision could result in teams boycotting Italian events. Although the FIA said its best legal advice was that the six would be acquitted, Mosley despatched an urgent memorandum on the difficulties posed by Italian law, as this was now being applied, to the Automobile Club of Italy and requested it be transmitted to the Italian Government.

'This is a uniquely Italian problem requiring a uniquely Italian solution,' said Mosley. 'Whatever the outcome, no other country is involved and the Formula 1 World Championship will not be affected; nor will the World and European Rally Championships.'

Many teams expressed support for the FIA's prompt action. 'We will be looking to the FIA for guidance,' said Ian Phillips, Jordan's commercial director, 'but the gut feeling is, as things stand, that we couldn't risk racing in Italy. There are far greater implications than simply those for the competing teams. It is not really an issue which the teams can handle on their own. Max Mosley has very quickly taken a stance on the matter, as we would have expected, and we are confident in his ability to sort it out.'

Ken Tyrrell added: 'Williams are arguably the most reliable team in the history of F1. If it can happen to them, what chance is there for the rest of us?'

In the run-up to the trial – staged in 1997 in a small courthouse at Imola – renewed speculation over the cause of the accident was stoked by the emergence of hitherto unpublished photographic evidence which seemed to show that the

Brazilian driver could have damaged his car by running over debris on the circuit moments before his accident.

A photograph taken by Frenchman Paul-Henri Cahier shows Senna approaching the Tamburello turn – with the left-hand wheels of the FW16 apparently on course to run over a piece of debris on the circuit. Its colour suggested that this could have come from J.J. Lehto's Benetton which had stalled on the starting grid just before the green light and was rammed by Pedro Lamy's Lotus. As a result of that accident, the safety car had been deployed to slow the field for the first five laps of the race while the collision site was cleared. Cahier had sent the photograph to both Williams and Renault immediately after the crash in the hope that they might find it useful, although the team steadfastly declined to comment on its significance.

An alternative theory to explain the crash was that Senna might have pressed too hard on cold tyres after several laps of running at a much-reduced speed behind the safety car. F1 tyres depend on heat build-up from vigorous use to generate maximum grip. It is thought possible that when the race was continued, the FW16's cool tyres could have been seriously lacking in grip which created a situation beyond even Senna's control.

Safety car driver Max Angelelli was known to be concerned that the modest Opel allocated to the task was not capable of running quickly enough to lead a Grand Prix field even running at much reduced speed. 'It was a nightmare,' he told the *Sunday Times*. 'Several times Ayrton pulled up alongside me and waved for me to speed up. I could see from his eyes that he was very angry, very upset.'

Senna's state of mind that weekend was also being called into question. Stunned by Roland Ratzenberger's fatal accident the previous day, inwardly suspicious that Michael Schumacher's Benetton had some sort of illegal control system, and reputedly bristling after an argument with his brother Leo over his young model girlfriend Adriane Galisteu – of whom his family disapproved – the Brazilian driver might quite simply have made a disastrous driving error.

The investigation ground on.

*Senna at Imola, 1994, that fateful weekend.* (Formula One Pictures)

but everything seemed to go wrong, almost from the outset. A succession of trifling technical problems, handling difficulties with the car and two highly public collisions with Schumacher's Benetton-Renault at Silverstone and Monza put the kibosh on Damon's hopes. He won at Buenos Aires, Imola, Hungaroring and Adelaide. But it wasn't enough. Hill had become demoralised and it showed.

---

## Villeneuve brought a fresh open-minded approach to F1

---

More worryingly, the downside of his performance prompted Williams to make alternative arrangements for 1997 when Hill's contract would expire. They did a deal to recruit German driver Heinz-Harald Frentzen, not for one second believing that Hill would get his head together in brilliant style to win the 1996 title.

During 1995 David Coulthard had proved himself to be a formidable driver. But after he was defeated in a straight fight against Schumacher's Benetton at Hockenheim, the Williams management began to think twice as to whether he too was made of the right stuff. They decided he wasn't. Despite scoring his first Grand Prix win at Estoril, the Scot would not be retained for 1996.

Simultaneously, Williams were being pressured by F1's Mr Fixit, Bernie Ecclestone, to give a test to the reign-ing Indycar Champion Jacques Villeneuve, son of the late great Ferrari driver Gilles Villeneuve.

That Villeneuve got the job was no surprise. Coulthard duly took up a pre-arranged vacancy in the McLaren-Mercedes squad, while Villeneuve went on to enjoy more than 10,000 kilometres of pre-season testing with Williams. Small wonder, some thought, that he planted the new FW18 on pole position for the first Australian Grand Prix to be held at Melbourne in March 1996.

Villeneuve had four wins during his freshman season. His first was the European Grand Prix at the new Nurburgring which he clinched in a split-second finish ahead of Michael Schumacher's Ferrari. Thus was a new F1 folk hero created.

An independent-minded non-conformist, Villeneuve brought a refreshingly open-minded approach to F1. He was a racer through and through, never cowed by his rivals – and in 1996 he certainly gave his team-mate a run for his money.

Hill had started the 1996 season noting that since 1990 every driver who had won the opening race of the season had gone on to win the Championship. 'It is a tradition I intend to continue,' he said after scoring a rather fortuitous victory at Melbourne when Villeneuve was slowed by fluctuating oil pressure.

Hill was as good as his word. If there

*Quiet moment before the 1995 Australian Grand Prix, a race Hill won with a display of confidence he would carry over to the following year.* (Formula One Pictures)

was any tinge of disappointment that season it was probably the failure to win the Monaco Grand Prix, an event in which his father Graham had triumphed no fewer than five times. Damon started from second place on the grid and accelerated into an immediate lead only to lose what looked a certain victory when his Renault engine suffered a rare failure.

Williams contributed their own bombshell too of course. The news – announced at the very height of Hill's title challenge – that his contract would not be renewed for 1997, was a tough blow to field. But, well used to life's little knocks, he shrugged aside the humiliation as best he could, proved the doubters wrong in magnificent style, and then relished his role as F1's first second-generation World Champion. It was an achievement difficult to imagine being repeated.

The 1997 season was a two-horse race between Jacques Villeneuve and Michael Schumacher. It ended with Williams still decisively on top, clinching the record ninth Constructors' Championship, and Villeneuve taking the Drivers' crown – the most hard won and satisfying title, said Frank, since Alan Jones won in 1980. Michael Schumacher was left to repent at leisure for the dubious piece of driving which beached his own title hopes in a Jerez gravel trap and damaged, perhaps

*Jacques Villeneuve joined the team for 1996. He is seen here with Jock Clear and Williams operations engineer James Robinson (right).* (Formula One Pictures)

for ever, his hero status among the Ferrari faithful.

Jacques Villeneuve had not needed much help in seeing off his new partner, ex-Sauber driver Heinz-Harald Frentzen. 'HH' had arrived at Williams preceded by a reputation for outstanding natural speed in the junior formulae where he had frequently outrun Michael Schumacher (also at one point also dating Corinna Betsch, who in 1995 married the double World Champion). But even before the first race, Frentzen had raised Patrick Head's blood pressure by creasing one of the FW19 chassis over a kerb during testing at Magny-Cours. And things didn't improve for a while.

Villeneuve started the year as odds-on title favourite. Despite a strong challenge from Schumacher and the re-born Ferrari equipe, he displayed brilliant form right through to his home race in Canada where he unaccountably spun off on the second lap. It was the start of a troubled period for him. Despite wins at Silverstone and Hungaroring, he wobbled quite badly during the summer months, then picked up the pace with a vengeance in the closing races.

Jacques's long-time manager Craig Pollock tells me this tendency towards a mid-season slump has been a feature of his career to date: 'But he always

*Villeneuve leads from the start of the 1997 San Marino Grand Prix, but team-mate Heinz-Harald Frentzen (left) eventually won the race.* (ICN UK Bureau)

comes back strongly'. Pollock was right. When the chips were down in the final sprint to the title, he never wavered.

But by the end of the 1997 season Williams was already hearing worrying rumours to the effect that Jacques might have decided to switch to the planned Reynard F1 operation for 1999. This new team, bankrolled by British American Tobacco with a £250 million budget over five years, was the brainchild of Reynard, the Bicester racing cars constructor, and Craig Pollock. So with Villeneuve's plans uncertain after his current contract with Williams expired at the end of 1998, Williams took the unprecedented step of testing four young drivers at Estoril in November 1997.

Colombia's Juan Pablo Montoya, French F3 ace Nicolas Minassian and F3000 drivers Max Wilson (a Brazilian, despite his name) and Soheil Ayari from France shared time at the wheel of a Williams FW19 over two days.

'We are very impressed with the way in which all four drivers conducted themselves,' said James Robinson, Williams's senior operations engineer. 'Taking into account each driver's previous experience and circuit knowledge, they did an excellent job.

'We were amazed by the level all four of them were at, particularly their level of awareness at what was involved in operating the cars. All could explain what the car was doing, and spotted things on the dashboard and from their pit signals. They were not under pressure to produce absolute times as we were assessing them in 13 separate categories.

'They were also very different characters, ranging from Wilson who is quiet to Montoya who is outgoing. They did extremely well and it was quite an eye-opener for us all.' Williams was expected to select its new test driver for the 1998 season from among this talented quartet.

# Chapter 6

# Race weekend

Preparations for a Grand Prix weekend are continuous at Williams Grand Prix Engineering. Even after the cars have been returned from the final race of the season, team manager Dickie Stanford and his colleagues find their thoughts turning to how they might tackle the jobs next

*They like what they see. Alain Prost and Renault Sport's Christian Contzen, Germany, 1993.* (Formula One Pictures)

year, how their operational techniques might be streamlined still further.

Stanford is a typically committed member of the F1 fraternity whose enthusiasm for motor racing is unstinting. 'I arrived in motor racing without any special qualifications,' he recalls, 'simply through helping a friend race his Formula Ford car back in the 1970s and this eventually led to a full-time job with his team.

---

## *It takes nearly a week to box up all the spares before a race*

---

'I worked up through Formula Ford and FF2000 before joining the Tiga F3 team in the early 1980s. I dropped out of motor racing for a year, but returned soon afterwards to work for the Ralt F2 team in the days when they had Mike Thackwell, Jonathan Palmer and Roberto Moreno driving.

'I was then invited to join Williams, spent two years on the test team and then got promotion to chief mechanic in 1990. Five years later, Frank and Patrick appointed me team manager.'

For the European races, the team's three Renault turbo transporters are pressed into action, but for the fly-aways – races on the other side of the world – the logistical challenge is

*Hill congratulates Villeneuve after being almost beaten by his new team-mate in the opening race of the 1996 season at Melbourne.* (Formula One Pictures)

more complex. Cars have to be stripped and re-prepared following the previous race, with one eye always on the clock. They must be delivered to Stansted airport for loading onto one of the three Boeing 747 cargo freighters organised by the F1 Constructors' Association. The timetable is rigid.

'For most of the fly-aways we take three cars and around 18 tons of spare parts packed in between 65 and 70 steel-sided containers,' says Dickie Stanford. 'It takes three or four people the best part of a week simply to box up all the contents before we take them to the airport.'

For a long haul race most of the team personnel will fly out on a Sunday before the race to set up the pit garage and unpack the cars and spares. They will be joined by the engineers and PR and media people on the Tuesday.

On the face of it, the European races are more straightforward in the sense that the team has more control over the destiny of its precious equipment. Early on the Monday prior to a Grand Prix, the first three Williams transporters leave Grove heading for Portsmouth, Le Havre or Dover – depending on the eventual destination – from where they will cross the channel, arriving at the circuit concerned on Tuesday night or Wednesday morning. (The exception is Monaco, where the race programme starts on the Thursday not Friday.)

The round trip to the most distant European race, the Portuguese Grand

*Preparing Hill for action, Portuguese Grand Prix, 1996.* (Formula One Pictures)

Prix at Estoril, is 2,946 miles, and takes two days seven hours each way. Six drivers share the driving, two each in both of the 38 tonne articulated trucks and the 24 tonne rigid truck. One artic accommodates the team's three cars for that race weekend, the second is the team office and technical component sub-assembly area (a portable factory, if you like) and the third transporter carries all the extra spares and components.

## Frentzen likes a large plate of mashed potato before a race

In addition, there is an articulated truck from which all the technical engine maintenance over the weekend is conducted, plus a motorhome for both Renault and the Williams team. The Williams motorhome, effectively Frank's private inner sanctum, is equipped with an electric lift attached to its main staircase to enable his wheelchair to be winched inside.

The transporters are usually in their allotted place within the F1 paddock by noon on Wednesday. The 43 team personnel use charters arranged by FOCA to fly out first thing on Thursday morning. A fleet of hire cars and mini-vans are waiting at the airport concerned – for Monaco Williams hire 12 scooters and three quad bikes, plus helmets – and, by lunchtime on Thursday, the mechanics and engineers are all at the track, the cars unloaded and positioned in their allocated pit garages.

In 1997 the Williams squad was supplemented by around 15 engineers from Renault. It is expected that the same number will be in attendance in 1998 when the team will continue to use the French V10 engines, even though these will be badged Mecachrome after the Renault sub-contractor officially supplying them.

Rather than collect and deliver the engines from the race, Williams has traditionally obtained and returned its V10s from Renault Sport's Paris base. The engines are installed in the cars at Grove – and fired up to check that they are functioning correctly – before the cars depart for the next Grand Prix. Usually all three team cars, the two race chassis and the spare, have a routine engine change on Saturday evening, but if there is even a hint of trouble on Friday, fresh engines will be installed on Friday night as well.

Friday free practice is from 11.00am–12 noon and from 1.00–2.00pm. The Williams drivers will tend to take things easily during the first stint, preferring to be late out onto the circuit in the hope that rivals will have cleaned up the residual dust and dirt which invariably coats the track surface. Race preparation is the key note on Friday. Villeneuve and Frentzen generally use only one set of tyres each. The 1998 F1 regulations permit ten sets of dry weather tyres per

*Frentzen, the cheerful and mild-mannered German who clinched Williams's record ninth Constructors' title in 1997.* (ICN UK Bureau)

*The team's motorhome alongside its Renault and Rothmans stablemates.* (Formula One Pictures)

car per race weekend, so there is obviously a premium on retaining as many fresh sets as possible for Saturday afternoon's qualifying session and Sunday's race. In addition, up to seven sets of rain tyres are allowed per car.

After each practice session, Villeneuve and Frentzen will retire to the office in the transporter to analyse their performances with their individual race engineers, respectively Jock Clear and Tim Preston. Subtle changes may be made to the cars in preparation for the next session, then on Saturday morning the tempo tends to pick up as the team starts thinking in terms of the best qualifying set-up.

Saturday free practice takes place from 9.00–9.45am, then from 10.15–11.00am. A two hour break

follows after which qualifying, the key to grid positions, runs from 1.00–2.00pm with each competitor permitted 12 timed laps. After that comes more de-briefing with the drivers while the mechanics knuckle down to change the engines for the race. Sandwiched between these flurries of high octane activity, drivers must also fraternise with the team's guests and sponsors, attend press conferences, service their own national media, sign autographs, and smile, smile, smile.

Like an army, of course, F1 crews tend to march on their stomachs. Williams has its own contracted catering company run by long-time fan and amateur hillclimb competitor Paul Edwards, aka The Fat Controller for reasons which reflect his role as a

*Paul Edwards and his team face their own pressures, serving 1,500 meals over a race weekend.* (Formula One Pictures)

trencherman of considerable taste and discernment!

While the action takes place on the circuit, Paul and his staff of two are busy rustling up on-circuit breakfasts for the mechanics in addition to VIP lunches and dinners for influential sponsors and business partners of the team, many of whom attend one or more races during the season.

Edwards, a former Cunard liner chef, caters for various branches of motorsport worldwide. Arriving for a Grand Prix he tends to shop locally, although certain staple ingredients – 'like bacon, black pudding and thick-cut Oxford marmalade' – are shipped out from Britain with the team. Over the course of three days, the Williams catering department can serve up to 1500

meals, so Paul's crew are under as much pressure in their own way as the race team mechanics.

For the drivers, of course, full English fry-ups tend to be off the menu, even though during Damon Hill's time with the team he could often be seen casting envious sideways glances as the mechanics tucked into their early morning 'full house.' He liked his morning porridge, as did Coulthard. Frentzen is partial to a large plate of mashed potato rather than pasta before a race, while Villeneuve tucks into egg bread with syrup. Senna was as fastidious about food as he was about racing, recalls Edwards. 'He was so obsessed with hygiene he would have his vegetables re-washed in bottled mineral water.'

Damon Hill's physical fitness regime

during his 1996 Championship year was pretty representative of the regimes adopted by all top-line F1 drivers. He credited much of his on-track consistency to the punishing programme of physical training. The man pushing him hard behind the scenes was his personal trainer Erwin Gollner who started work for the British driver in December 1995 and still works for the Williams team.

## A race driver's body must be as well tuned as his car

Previously Gollner had worked in Formula 3000 and later with the Scuderia Italia and Minardi F1 teams. It is rumoured that Michael Schumacher made a strong bid to secure his services for the 1997 season.

When Gollner began working with Hill, he found that he was already in pretty good shape: 'I did a test on him to find out just how fit he was. This showed up a few weak points where he was not quite 100 per cent, so I devised a new programme for him.'

Hill was a willing student who enjoyed his training. 'Nobody likes training every day, but Damon did all the work I asked him to do. If he was alone at home, he would work out five days a week for between two and three hours each day. But if I visited him in Dublin, or if he came to me in Salzburg, then he would train for up to six hours a day.'

The key to top notch fitness is, according to Gollner, a well balanced programme combining work-outs with endurance training. Damon's favourite form of exercise is the rowing machine, which might have something to do with the fact that his parents Bette and Graham were both competitive rowers. To this day, Damon's helmet carries the distinctive vertical stripes of the London Rowing Club.

Gollner is also insistent that a racing driver's body must be as finely tuned as his car. For both, the right fuel is of paramount importance. 'When we started working together, I went to Damon's home, checked out his kitchen and went through a dietary programme with him. So he was not allowed to eat what he liked.

'At the race track I prepared muesli for his breakfast, but at lunchtime and dinner Hilary, the Williams chef, cooked his meal as she is a much better cook than I am. But I would tell her what to prepare.'

Others have it easier on race weekend. Williams purchases tickets in the five-star Paddock Club for many VIPs. The Paddock Club, run by Paddy McNally's Geneva-based AllSport Management, provides deluxe catering and viewing facilities for clients of all F1 teams on a regular basis at every race.

Meanwhile the Williams motorsport press officer Ffiona Welford will be fielding a blizzard of media inquiries throughout the weekend, as well as regularly reporting back to the team's

*Drivers have one thing on their minds – winning races.* (Formula One Pictures)

headquarters where media manager Jane Gorard and media executive Lindsay Morle will be holding the fort. Ffiona will also control access to the drivers for one-to-one interviews at the circuits, something which has to be arranged well in advance as the drivers jealously guard whatever free time is available to them.

Sunday morning brings a further intensification of pressure on the drivers, mechanics and engineers. There is a half-hour warm-up session during which the race set-up of the cars

*The Paddock Club offers top class hospitality for F1 High Rollers.* (Formula One Pictures)

is checked and final decisions will be taken over the crucial matter of re-fuelling strategy. Since the introduction of in-race refuelling in 1994, this is often where races are won and lost.

The image of a Formula 1 driver as a dashing philanderer is firmly rooted in history – helped perhaps by the droves of leggy beauties decorating the Grand Prix scene. But it's not true, certainly as far as race weekends are concerned. These men may have one thing on their minds, but it's winning not womanising. By the time the team's debrief has been completed on Saturday afternoon the drivers are exhausted. They may go for a run, a work-out or a sauna on the night prior to the race. Most will then have a light meal and be in bed by 10pm.

For the mechanics too there is little free time. Many nights they will eat at the circuit motorhome once their work is completed, on others they can be seen straggling back to the hotels as late as midnight. Some resilient survivors might make it to the bar for another hour, but most crash out. They will probably be called at 6.30am the following morning and, on race day at least, they will be on the road until after midnight when the F1 Constructors' Association charter plane finally deposits them at Luton, Stansted or some other semi-deserted UK airfield.

---

## Pitstops are F1's version of synchronised swimming

---

Throughout the weekend the cars' progress will be checked and monitored by engineers using sophisticated telemetry systems. These enable computer read-outs of acceleration, braking, cornering forces and degrees of throttle opening to be monitored in detail from the back of the pit garage. They are not only a means of double-checking whether or not the cars' technical systems are operating to optimum effect, but also allow the engineers to get comparative 'traces' showing any variations between the performance of the two drivers.

Of course, all this detailed information can be rendered totally worthless if the wrong tyre choice is made on race day. That means that there is a premium on accurate weather forecasting. The Williams team subscribes to a quite costly satellite system to give them all the right information on an hourly basis. In that connection, it is perhaps best not to mention the 1997 Monaco Grand Prix where both Villeneuve's and Frentzen's cars started the race on dry weather slicks – in a monsoon. The team had reportedly been assured that this was nothing more than a passing shower . . .

At 11.00am on race morning comes the drivers' briefing. Attendance is mandatory and heavy fines can be inflicted on those who miss it, or even arrive late. In reality, there is little chance of that, since each team has one member deputed to make sure that the competitors are on parade at the right moment.

About 40 minutes before the start of the race, the drivers begin to prepare for action. The pit lane exit opens with half an hour to go, at which point the drivers complete at least one warm-up lap before taking their places on the grid.

The cars will then be fired up, the field accelerates away on its formation lap, before pausing briefly for the starting signal to be given. Once the pack is away, with the leading bunch jostling for position into the first corner, the engineers and team management can only watch and monitor the proceedings. Their job is now done. From here on, everything rests on the drivers.

*Patrick Head standing with his wife Beatise outside the Williams team motorhome. (Formula One Pictures)*

Until the first refuelling stop, that is.

The Williams team spends many hours on empty test tracks honing its pit stop technique to near-perfection. This slickly choreographed performance is F1's equivalent of synchronised swimming. In the few seconds the car is stationary for refuelling and fresh tyres, a total of 21 perfectly drilled team personnel work amid pressure cooker intensity, but in harmony. The moment the car stops, the driver keeps his right foot firmly on the brake and the jacks go under the front and rear of the car. One mechanic per wheel attaches the compressed air gun to the central nut locating that wheel on its hub, another removes the discarded wheel and a third offers up its replacement for the wheel gun to immediately tighten.

Simultaneously, two more mechanics are in control of the refuelling line which attaches to a quick-release connection on the side of the fuel cell, with a third operating the refuelling rig itself. From the front of the car, the chief mechanic keeps overall control of the proceedings, only signalling the driver back into the race when he is satisfied that all the various tasks have been completed with flawless precision. From the moment the car rolls to a halt to the time it is signalled back into the fray, hopefully no more than eight seconds will have passed.

The cars which survive to the finish of the race, streaked with oil and

*Races can be won or lost at a pit stop. The Williams pit crew swings into action at the French Grand Prix.* (Formula One Pictures)

*Transporting F1 cars is an art form.*
(Formula One Pictures)

*Resting place. Last year's cars get pride of place in the Williams collection at the Grove headquarters.* (Formula One Pictures)

grime, will be directed immediately into the parc ferme where nobody from the teams is allowed access to them for some time after the race. During this period they are checked in detail for conformity with the technical regulations and random fuel samples will be taken to ensure that these match the official specifications.

Yet almost before the exhaust notes are stilled, the Williams mechanics will be working flat-out to pack the transporters for the journey home. 'There may be time for ten minutes' rest and a cup of tea, then it's all hands to the pump,' says Dickie Stanford. 'We aim to have the transporters completely loaded up by the time the lads leave the circuit for the late evening charter flight home.'

By Tuesday morning, the Williams transporters are back inside the security gates at Grove, the cars unloaded. And the whole process starts again from square one in preparation for the following race.

# Appendix 1

# Williams – race results

The accompanying results table includes all the Formula 1 race results achieved by Williams-entered Grand Prix cars from Piers Courage's debut at the wheel of the ex-works Brabham in the 1969 Race of Champions through to the final round of the 1997 season.

*Key to abbreviations:*

R – retired; N – did not start;
C – non classified; F – fatal accident;
Q – did not qualify; D – disqualified.

## 1969

16 Mar   Race of Champions, Brands Hatch
  P. Courage    Brabham-Cosworth BT26    R
30 Apr   International Trophy, Silverstone
  P. Courage    Brabham-Cosworth BT26    5
4 May   SPANISH GP, Montjuich Park
  P. Courage    Brabham-Cosworth BT26    R
18 May   MONACO GP, Monte Carlo
  P. Courage    Brabham-Cosworth BT26A    2
21 Jun   DUTCH GP, Zandvoort
  P. Courage    Brabham-Cosworth BT26A    R

6 Jul   FRENCH GP, Clermont-Ferrand
  P. Courage    Brabham-Cosworth BT26A    R
19 Jul   BRITISH GP, Silverstone
  P. Courage    Brabham-Cosworth BT26A    5
3 Aug   GERMAN GP, Nurburgring
  P. Courage    Brabham-Cosworth BT26A    R
7 Sep   ITALIAN GP, Monza
  P. Courage    Brabham-Cosworth BT26A    5
20 Sep   CANADIAN GP, Mosport Park
  P. Courage    Brabham-Cosworth BT26A    R
5 Oct   UNITED STATES GP, Watkins Glen
  P. Courage    Brabham-Cosworth BT26A    2
19 Oct   MEXICAN GP, Mexico City
  P. Courage    Brabham-Cosworth BT26A    10

## 1970

7 Mar   SOUTH AFRICAN GP, Kyalami
  P. Courage    de Tomaso-Cosworth 505    R
19 Apr   SPANISH GP, Jarama
  P. Courage    de Tomaso-Cosworth 505    N
26 Apr   International Trophy, Silverstone
  P. Courage    de Tomaso-Cosworth 505    3
10 May   MONACO GP, Monte Carlo
  P. Courage    de Tomaso-Cosworth 505    C
7 Jun   BELGIAN GP, Spa-Francorchamps
  P. Courage    de Tomaso-Cosworth 505    R
21 Jun   DUTCH GP, Zandvoort
  P. Courage    de Tomaso-Cosworth 505    F

19 Jul BRITISH GP, Brands Hatch
B. Redman de Tomaso-Cosworth 505 N
2 Aug GERMAN GP, Hockenheim
B. Redman de Tomaso-Cosworth 505 Q
16 Aug AUSTRIAN GP, Osterreichring
T. Schenken de Tomaso-Cosworth 505 R
6 Sep ITALIAN GP, Monza
T. Schenken de Tomaso-Cosworth 505 R
20 Sep CANADIAN GP, St. Jovite
T. Schenken de Tomaso-Cosworth 505 C
4 Oct UNITED STATES GP, Watkins Glen
T. Schenken de Tomaso-Cosworth 505 R

# 1971

24 Jan ARGENTINE GP, Buenos Aires
H. Pescarolo March-Cosworth 701 2
6 Mar SOUTH AFRICAN GP, Kyalami
H. Pescarolo March-Cosworth 701 11
21 Mar Race of Champions, Brands Hatch
R. Peterson March-Cosworth 711 R
R. Allen March-Cosworth 701 6
28 Mar Questor GP, Ontario Motor Speedway
H. Pescarolo March-Cosworth 711 20
D. Bell March-Cosworth 701 15
9 Apr International Trophy, Oulton Park
C. Williams March-Cosworth 701 N
18 Apr SPANISH GP, Montjuich Park
H. Pescarolo March-Cosworth 711 R
23 May MONACO GP, Monte Carlo
H. Pescarolo March-Cosworth 711 8
13 Jun Rindt Memorial Trophy, Hockenheim
R. Allen March-Cosworth 701 R
20 Jun DUTCH GP, Zandvoort
H. Pescarolo March-Cosworth 711 13
4 Jul FRENCH GP, Circuit Paul Ricard
H. Pescarolo March-Cosworth 711 R
17 Jul BRITISH GP, Silverstone
H. Pescarolo March-Cosworth 711 4
1 Aug GERMAN GP, Nurburgring
H. Pescarolo March-Cosworth 711 R
15 Aug AUSTRIAN GP, Osterreichring
H. Pescarolo March-Cosworth 711 6
21 Aug Gold Cup, Oulton Park
H. Pescarolo March-Cosworth 711 R
5 Sep ITALIAN GP, Monza
H. Pescarolo March-Cosworth 711 R

19 Sep CANADIAN GP, Mosport Park
H. Pescarolo March-Cosworth 711 N
3 Oct UNITED STATES GP, Watkins Glen
H. Pescarolo March-Cosworth 711 R
24 Oct Victory Race, Brands Hatch
H. Pescarolo March-Cosworth 711 R

# 1972

23 Jan ARGENTINE GP, Buenos Aires
H. Pescarolo March-Cosworth 721 8
4 Mar SOUTH AFRICAN GP, Kyalami
H. Pescarolo March-Cosworth 721 11
C. Pace March-Cosworth 711 17
30 Mar BRAZILIAN GP, Interlagos
H. Pescarolo March-Cosworth 721 R
C. Pace March-Cosworth 711 R
23 Apr International Trophy, Silverstone
H. Pescarolo March-Cosworth 721 R
1 May SPANISH GP, Jarama
H. Pescarolo March-Cosworth 721 11
C. Pace March-Cosworth 711 6
14 May MONACO GP, Monte Carlo
H. Pescarolo March-Cosworth 721 R
C. Pace March-Cosworth 711 17
4 Jun BELGIAN GP, Nivelles
H. Pescarolo March-Cosworth 721 C
C. Pace March-Cosworth 711 5
18 Jun REPUBLICA GP, Vallelunga
H. Pescarolo March-Cosworth 711 R
2 Jul FRENCH GP, Clermont-Ferrand
H. Pescarolo March-Cosworth 721 N
C. Pace March-Cosworth 711 R
15 Jul BRITISH GP, Brands Hatch
H. Pescarolo Politoys-Cosworth FX3 R
C. Pace March-Cosworth 711 R
30 Jul GERMAN GP, Nurburgring
H. Pescarolo March-Cosworth 721 R
C. Pace March-Cosworth 711 C
13 Aug AUSTRIAN GP, Osterreichring
H. Pescarolo March-Cosworth 721 N
C. Pace March-Cosworth 711 C
28 Aug Rothmans 50,000 Formule Libre race,
Brands Hatch
H. Pescarolo March-Cosworth 721 3
10 Sep ITALIAN GP, Monza
H. Pescarolo March-Cosworth 721 R
C. Pace March-Cosworth 711 R

24 Sep   CANADIAN GP, Mosport Park
   H. Pescarolo  March-Cosworth 721       13
   C. Pace       March-Cosworth 711        9
8  Oct   UNITED STATES GP, Watkins Glen
   H. Pescarolo  March-Cosworth 721       14
   C. Pace       March-Cosworth 711        R
22 Oct   Challenge Trophy race, Brands Hatch
   H. Pescarolo  March-Cosworth 721        R
   C. Amon       Politoys-Cosworth FX3      N

# 1973

28 Jan   ARGENTINE GP, Buenos Aires
   H. Ganley     Iso-Marlboro-Cosworth FX3B C
   G. Galli      Iso-Marlboro-Cosworth FX3B R
11 Feb   BRAZILIAN GP, Interlagos
   H. Ganley     Iso-Marlboro-Cosworth FX3B 7
   G. Galli      Iso-Marlboro-Cosworth FX3B 9
3  Mar   SOUTH AFRICAN GP, Kyalami
   H. Ganley     Iso-Marlboro-Cosworth FX3B 10
   J. Pretorius  Iso-Marlboro-Cosworth FX3B R
18 Mar   Race of Champions, Brands Hatch
   H. Ganley     Iso-Marlboro-Cosworth FX3B R
   T. Trimmer    Iso-Marlboro-Cosworth FX3B 4
7  Apr   International Trophy, Silverstone
   H. Ganley     Iso-Marlboro-Cosworth FX3B R
29 Apr   SPANISH GP, Montjuich
   H. Ganley     Iso-Marlboro-Cosworth IR    R
   G. Galli      Iso-Marlboro-Cosworth IR    11
20 May   BELGIAN GP, Zolder
   H. Ganley     Iso-Marlboro-Cosworth IR    R
   G. Galli      Iso-Marlboro-Cosworth IR    R
3  Jun   MONACO GP, Monte Carlo
   H. Ganley     Iso-Marlboro-Cosworth IR    R
   G. Galli      Iso-Marlboro-Cosworth IR    R
17 Jun   SWEDISH GP, Anderstorp
   H. Ganley     Iso-Marlboro-Cosworth IR    11
   T. Belso      Iso-Marlboro-Cosworth IR    N
1  Jul   FRENCH GP, Circuit Paul Ricard
   H. Ganley     Iso-Marlboro-Cosworth IR    14
   H. Pescarolo  Iso-Marlboro-Cosworth IR    R
14 Jul   BRITISH GP, Silverstone
   H. Ganley     Iso-Marlboro-Cosworth IR    9
   G. McRae      Iso-Marlboro-Cosworth IR    R
29 Jul   DUTCH GP, Zandvoort
   H. Ganley     Iso-Marlboro-Cosworth IR    9
   G. v Lennep   Iso-Marlboro-Cosworth IR    6

5  Aug   GERMAN GP, Nurburgring
   H. Ganley     Iso-Marlboro-Cosworth IR    N
   H. Pescarolo  Iso-Marlboro-Cosworth IR    10
19 Aug   AUSTRIAN GP, Osterreichring
   H. Ganley     Iso-Marlboro-Cosworth IR    C
   G. v Lennep   Iso-Marlboro-Cosworth IR    9
9  Sep   ITALIAN GP, Monza
   H. Ganley     Iso-Marlboro-Cosworth IR    C
   G. v Lennep   Iso-Marlboro-Cosworth IR    R
23 Sep   CANADIAN GP, Mosport Park
   H. Ganley     Iso-Marlboro-Cosworth IR    6
   T. Schenken   Iso-Marlboro-Cosworth IR    14
7  Oct   UNITED STATES GP, Watkins Glen
   H. Ganley     Iso-Marlboro-Cosworth IR    12
   J. Ickx       Iso-Marlboro-Cosworth IR    7

# 1974

13 Jan   ARGENTINE GP, Buenos Aires
   A. Merzario   Iso-Marlboro-Cosworth FW    R
27 Jan   BRAZILIAN GP, Interlagos
   A. Merzario   Iso-Marlboro-Cosworth FW    R
3  Feb   Presidente Medici GP, Brasilia
   A. Merzario   Iso-Marlboro-Cosworth FW    3
30 Mar   SOUTH AFRICAN GP, Kyalami
   A. Merzario   Iso-Marlboro-Cosworth FW    6
   T. Belso      Iso-Marlboro-Cosworth FW    R
28 Apr   SPANISH GP, Jarama
   A. Merzario   Iso-Marlboro-Cosworth FW    R
   T. Belso      Iso-Marlboro-Cosworth FW    Q
12 May   BELGIAN GP, Nivelles
   A. Merzario   Iso-Marlboro-Cosworth FW    R
   G. v Lennep   Iso-Marlboro-Cosworth FW    14
26 May   MONACO GP, Monte Carlo
   A. Merzario   Iso-Marlboro-Cosworth FW    R
9  Jun   SWEDISH GP, Anderstorp
   T. Belso      Iso-Marlboro-Cosworth FW    8
   R. Robarts    Iso-Marlboro-Cosworth FW    N
23 Jun   DUTCH GP, Zandvoort
   A. Merzario   Iso-Marlboro-Cosworth FW    R
   G. v Lennep   Iso-Marlboro-Cosworth FW    Q
7  Jul   FRENCH GP, Dijon-Prenois
   A. Merzario   Iso-Marlboro-Cosworth FW    9
   J-P. Jabouille Iso-Marlboro-Cosworth FW   Q
20 Jul   BRITISH GP, Brands Hatch
   A. Merzario   Iso-Marlboro-Cosworth FW    R
   T. Belso      Iso-Marlboro-Cosworth FW    Q

4 Aug   GERMAN GP, Nurburgring
A. Merzario   Iso-Marlboro-Cosworth FW   R
J. Laffite       Iso-Marlboro-Cosworth FW   R
18 Aug   AUSTRIAN GP, Osterreichring
A. Merzario   Iso-Marlboro-Cosworth FW   R
J. Laffite       Iso-Marlboro-Cosworth FW   C
8 Sep   ITALIAN GP, Monza
A. Merzario   Iso-Marlboro-Cosworth FW   4
J. Laffite       Iso-Marlboro-Cosworth FW   R
22 Sep   CANADIAN GP, Mosport Park
A. Merzario   Iso-Marlboro-Cosworth FW   R
J. Laffite       Iso-Marlboro-Cosworth FW   R
6 Oct   UNITED STATES GP, Watkins Glen
A. Merzario   Iso-Marlboro-Cosworth FW   R
J. Laffite       Iso-Marlboro-CosworthFW   R

# 1975

12 Jan     ARGENTINE GP, Buenos Aires
A. Merzario   Williams-Cosworth FW   C
J. Laffite       Williams-Cosworth FW   R
26 Jan     BRAZILIAN GP, Interlagos
A. Merzario   Williams-Cosworth FW   R
J. Laffite       Williams-Cosworth FW   11
1 Mar   SOUTH AFRICAN GP, Kyalami
A. Merzario   Williams-Cosworth FW   R
J. Laffite       Williams-Cosworth FW   C
16 Mar   Race of Champions, Brands Hatch
A. Merzario   Williams-Cosworth FW   7
M. Flammini   Williams-Cosworth FW   N
12 Apr   International Trophy, Silverstone
A. Merzario   Williams-Cosworth FW   N
27 Apr   SPANISH GP, Montjuich Park
A. Merzario   Williams-Cosworth FW   R
T. Brise        Williams-Cosworth FW   7
11 May   MONACO GP, Monte Carlo
A. Merzario   Williams-Cosworth FW   Q
J. Laffite       Williams-Cosworth FW   Q
25 May   BELGIAN GP, Zolder
A. Merzario   Williams-Cosworth FW   R
J. Laffite       Williams-Cosworth FW   R
8 Jun   SWEDISH GP, Anderstorp
D. Magee      Williams-Cosworth FW   14
I. Scheckter   Williams-Cosworth FW   R
22 Jun   DUTCH GP, Zandvoort
J. Laffite       Williams-Cosworth FW   R
I. Scheckter   Williams-Cosworth FW   12

6 Jul   FRENCH GP, Circuit Paul Ricard
F. Migault    Williams-Cosworth FW   N
J. Laffite       Williams-Cosworth FW   11
19 Jul   BRITISH GP, Silverstone
J. Laffite       Williams-Cosworth FW   R
3 Aug   GERMAN GP, Nurburgring
J. Laffite       Williams-Cosworth FW   2
I. Ashley     Williams-Cosworth FW   N
17 Aug   AUSTRIAN GP, Osterreichring
J. Laffite       Williams-Cosworth FW   R
J. Vonlanthen Williams-Cosworth FW   R
24 Aug   SWISS GP, Dijon-Prenois
J. Laffite       Williams-Cosworth FW   10
J. Vonlanthen Williams-Cosworth FW   14
7 Sep   ITALIAN GP, Monza
J. Laffite       Williams-Cosworth FW   R
R. Zorzi       Williams-Cosworth FW   14
5 Oct   UNITED STATES GP, Watkins Glen
J. Laffite       Williams-Cosworth FW   N
L. Lombardi   Williams-Cosworth FW   N

# 1976

25 Jan   BRAZILIAN GP, Interlagos
J. Ickx        Wolf-Williams-C'worth FW05   8
R. Zorzi      Wolf-Williams-C'worth FW05   9
6 Mar   SOUTH AFRICAN GP, Kyalami
J. Ickx        Wolf-Williams-C'worth FW05 16
M. Leclere   Wolf-Williams-C'worth FW05 13
14 Mar   Race of Champions, Brands Hatch
J. Ickx        Wolf-Williams-C'worth FW05   3
28 Mar   US GP WEST, Long Beach
J. Ickx        Wolf-Williams-C'worth FW05   Q
M. Leclere   Wolf-Williams-C'worth FW05   Q
11 Apr   International Trophy, Silverstone
J. Ickx        Wolf-Williams-C'worth FW05   R
M. Andretti   Wolf-Williams-C'worth FW05   7
2 May   SPANISH GP, Jarama
J. Ickx        Wolf-Williams-C'worth FW05   7
M. Leclere   Wolf-Williams-C'worth FW05 10
16 May   BELGIAN GP, Zolder
J. Ickx        Wolf-Williams-C'worth FW05   Q
M. Leclere   Wolf-Williams-C'worth FW05 11
30 May   MONACO GP, Monte Carlo
J. Ickx        Wolf-Williams-C'worth FW05   Q
M. Leclere   Wolf-Williams-C'worth FW05 11
13 Jun   SWEDISH GP, Anderstorp
M. Leclere   Wolf-Williams-C'worth FW05   R

4 Jul    FRENCH GP, Circuit Paul Ricard
  J. Ickx          Wolf-Williams-C'worth FW05 10
  M. Leclere      Wolf-Williams-C'worth FW05 13
18 Jul    BRITISH GP, Brands Hatch
  J. Ickx          Wolf-Williams-C'worth FW05 Q
1 Aug   GERMAN GP, Nurburgring
  A. Merzario  Wolf-Williams-C'worth FW05 R
15 Aug   AUSTRIAN GP, Osterreichring
  A. Merzario  Wolf-Williams-C'worth FW05 R
29 Aug   DUTCH GP, Zandvoort
  A. Merzario  Wolf-Williams-C'worth FW05 R
12 Sep   ITALIAN GP, Monza
  A. Merzario  Wolf-Williams-C'worth FW05 N
3 Oct   CANADIAN GP, Mosport Park
  A. Merzario  Wolf-Williams-C'worth FW05 R
  C. Amon       Wolf-Williams-C'worth FW05 N
10 Oct   UNITED STATES GP, Watkins Glen
  A. Merzario  Wolf-Williams-C'worth FW05 R
  W. Brown     Wolf-Williams-C'worth FW05 14
24 Oct   JAPANESE GP, Mount Fuji
  A. Merzario  Wolf-Williams-C'worth FW05 R
  H. Binder     Wolf-Williams-C'worth FW05 R

# 1977

8 May   SPANISH GP, Jarama
  P. Neve         March-Cosworth 761        12
5 Jun   BELGIAN GP, Zolder
  P. Neve         March-Cosworth 761        10
19 Jun   SWEDISH GP, Anderstorp
  P. Neve         March-Cosworth 761        15
3 Jul   FRENCH GP, Dijon-Prenois
  P. Neve         March-Cosworth 761        Q
16 Jul   BRITISH GP, Silverstone
  P. Neve         March-Cosworth 761        10
31 Jul   GERMAN GP, Hockenheim
  P. Neve         March-Cosworth 761        Q
14 Aug   AUSTRIAN GP, Osterreichring
  P. Neve         March-Cosworth 761        9
28 Aug   DUTCH GP, Zandvoort
  P. Neve         March-Cosworth 761        Q
11 Sep   ITALIAN GP, Monza
  P. Neve         March-Cosworth 761        7
2 Oct   UNITED STATES GP, Watkins Glen
  P. Neve         March-Cosworth 761        18
9 Oct   CANADIAN GP, Mosport Park
  P. Neve         March-Cosworth 761        R

# 1978

15 Jan    ARGENTINE GP, Buenos Aires
  A. Jones        Williams-Cosworth FW06    R
29 Jan   BRAZILIAN GP, Rio de Janeiro
  A. Jones        Williams-Cosworth FW06    11
4 Mar   SOUTH AFRICAN GP, Kyalami
  A. Jones        Williams-Cosworth FW06    4
2 Apr   US GP WEST, Long Beach
  A. Jones        Williams-Cosworth FW06    7
7 May   MONACO GP, Monte Carlo
  A. Jones        Williams-Cosworth FW06    R
21 May   BELGIAN GP, Zolder
  A. Jones        Williams-Cosworth FW06    10
4 Jun   SPANISH GP, Jarama
  A. Jones        Williams-Cosworth FW06    8
17 Jun   SWEDISH GP, Anderstorp
  A. Jones        Williams-Cosworth FW06    R
2 Jul   FRENCH GP, Circuit Paul Ricard
  A. Jones        Williams-Cosworth FW06    5
16 Jul   BRITISH GP, Brands Hatch
  A. Jones        Williams-Cosworth FW06    R
30 Jul    GERMAN GP, Hockenheim
  A. Jones        Williams-Cosworth FW06    R
13 Aug   AUSTRIAN GP, Osterreichring
  A. Jones        Williams-Cosworth FW06    R
27 Aug   DUTCH GP, Zandvoort
  A. Jones        Williams-Cosworth FW06    R
10 Sep   ITALIAN GP, Monza
  A. Jones        Williams-Cosworth FW06    13
1 Oct   UNITED STATES GP, Watkins Glen
  A. Jones        Williams-Cosworth FW06    2
8 Oct   CANADIAN GP, Montreal
  A. Jones        Williams-Cosworth FW06    9

# 1979

21 Jan   ARGENTINE GP, Buenos Aires
  A. Jones        Williams-Cosworth FW06    9
  C. Regazzoni  Williams-Cosworth FW06    10
4 Feb   BRAZILIAN GP, Interlagos
  A. Jones        Williams-Cosworth FW06    R
  C. Regazzoni  Williams-Cosworth FW06    15
3 Mar   SOUTH AFRICAN GP, Kyalami
  A. Jones        Williams-Cosworth FW06    R
  C. Regazzoni  Williams-Cosworth FW06    9
8 Apr   US GP WEST, Long Beach
  A. Jones        Williams-Cosworth FW06    3
  C. Regazzoni  Williams-Cosworth FW06    R

29 Apr    SPANISH GP, Jarama
    A. Jones       Williams-Cosworth FW07    R
    C. Regazzoni  Williams-Cosworth FW07    R
13 May    BELGIAN GP, Zolder
    A. Jones       Williams-Cosworth FW07    R
    C. Regazzoni  Williams-Cosworth FW07    R
27 May    MONACO GP, Monte Carlo
    A. Jones       Williams-Cosworth FW07    R
    C. Regazzoni  Williams-Cosworth FW07    2
1 Jul    FRENCH GP, Dijon-Prenois
    A. Jones       Williams-Cosworth FW07    4
    C. Regazzoni  Williams-Cosworth FW07    6
14 Jul    BRITISH GP, Silverstone
    A. Jones       Williams-Cosworth FW07    R
    C. Regazzoni  Williams-Cosworth FW07    1
29 Jul    GERMAN GP, Hockenheim
    A. Jones       Williams-Cosworth FW07    1
    C. Regazzoni  Williams-Cosworth FW07    2
12 Aug    AUSTRIAN GP, Osterreichring
    A. Jones       Williams-Cosworth FW07    1
    C. Regazzoni  Williams-Cosworth FW07    5
26 Aug    DUTCH GP, Zandvoort
    A. Jones       Williams-Cosworth FW07    1
    C. Regazzoni  Williams-Cosworth FW07    R
9 Sep    ITALIAN GP, Monza
    A. Jones       Williams-Cosworth FW07    9
    C. Regazzoni  Williams-Cosworth FW07    3
30 Sep    CANADIAN GP, Montreal
    A. Jones       Williams-Cosworth FW07    1
    C. Regazzoni  Williams-Cosworth FW07    3
7 Oct    UNITED STATES GP, Watkins Glen
    A. Jones       Williams-Cosworth FW07    R
    C. Regazzoni  Williams-Cosworth FW07    R

# 1980

13 Jan    ARGENTINE GP, Buenos Aires
    A. Jones       Williams-Cosworth FW07    1
    C. Reutemann Williams-Cosworth FW07B    R
27 Jan    BRAZILIAN GP, Interlagos
    A. Jones       Williams-Cosworth FW07B    3
    C. Reutemann Williams-Cosworth FW07B    R
1 Mar    SOUTH AFRICAN GP, Kyalami
    A. Jones       Williams-Cosworth FW07    R
    C. Reutemann Williams-Cosworth FW07B    5
30 Mar    US GP WEST, Long Beach
    A. Jones       Williams-Cosworth FW07B    R
    C. Reutemann Williams-Cosworth FW07B    R

4 May    BELGIAN GP, Zolder
    A. Jones       Williams-Cosworth FW07B    2
    C. Reutemann Williams-Cosworth FW07B    3
18 May    MONACO GP, Monte Carlo
    A. Jones       Williams-Cosworth FW07B    R
    C. Reutemann Williams-Cosworth FW07B    1
29 Jun    FRENCH GP, Circuit Paul Ricard
    A. Jones       Williams-Cosworth FW07B    1
    C. Reutemann Williams-Cosworth FW07B    6
13 Jul    BRITISH GP, Brands Hatch
    A. Jones       Williams-Cosworth FW07B    1
    C. Reutemann Williams-Cosworth FW07B    3
10 Aug    GERMAN GP, Hockenheim
    A. Jones       Williams-Cosworth FW07B    3
    C. Reutemann Williams-Cosworth FW07B    2
17 Aug    AUSTRIAN GP, Osterreichring
    A. Jones       Williams-Cosworth FW07B    2
    C. Reutemann Williams-Cosworth FW07B    3
31 Aug    DUTCH GP, Zandvoort
    A. Jones       Williams-Cosworth FW07B    11
    C. Reutemann Williams-Cosworth FW07B    4
14 Sep    ITALIAN GP, Imola
    A. Jones       Williams-Cosworth FW07B    2
    C. Reutemann Williams-Cosworth FW07B    3
28 Sep    CANADIAN GP, Montreal
    A. Jones       Williams-Cosworth FW07B    1
    C. Reutemann Williams-Cosworth FW07B    2
5 Oct    UNITED STATES GP, Watkins Glen
    A. Jones       Williams-Cosworth FW07B    1
    C. Reutemann Williams-Cosworth FW07B    2

# 1981

15 Mar    US GP WEST, Long Beach
    A. Jones       Williams-Cosworth FW07C    1
    C. Reutemann Williams-Cosworth FW07C    2
29 Mar    BRAZILIAN GP, Rio de Janeiro
    A. Jones       Williams-Cosworth FW07C    2
    C. Reutemann Williams-Cosworth FW07C    1
12 Apr    ARGENTINE GP, Buenos Aires
    A. Jones       Williams-Cosworth FW07C    4
    C. Reutemann Williams-Cosworth FW07C    2
3 May    SAN MARINO GP, Imola
    A. Jones       Williams-Cosworth FW07C    12
    C. Reutemann Williams-Cosworth FW07C    3
17 May    BELGIAN GP, Zolder
    A. Jones       Williams-Cosworth FW07C    R
    C. Reutemann Williams-Cosworth FW07C    1

31 May   MONACO GP, Monte Carlo
    A. Jones          Williams-Cosworth FW07C   2
    C. Reutemann Williams-Cosworth FW07C   R
21 Jun   SPANISH GP, Jarama
    A. Jones          Williams-Cosworth FW07C   7
    C. Reutemann Williams-Cosworth FW07C   4
5 Jul    FRENCH GP, Dijon Prenois
    A. Jones          Williams-Cosworth FW07C   17
    C. Reutemann Williams-Cosworth FW07C   10
18 Jul   BRITISH GP, Silverstone
    A. Jones          Williams-Cosworth FW07C   R
    C. Reutemann Williams-Cosworth FW07C   2
2 Aug   GERMAN GP, Hockenheim
    A. Jones          Williams-Cosworth FW07C   11
    C. Reutemann Williams-Cosworth FW07C   R
16 Aug   AUSTRIAN GP, Osterreichring
    A. Jones          Williams-Cosworth FW07C   4
    C. Reutemann Williams-Cosworth FW07C   5
30 Aug   DUTCH GP, Zandvoort
    A. Jones          Williams-Cosworth FW07C   3
    C. Reutemann Williams-Cosworth FW07C   R
13 Sep   ITALIAN GP, Monza
    A. Jones          Williams-Cosworth FW07C   2
    C. Reutemann Williams-Cosworth FW07C   3
27 Sep   CANADIAN GP, Montreal
    A. Jones          Williams-Cosworth FW07C   R
    C. Reutemann Williams-Cosworth FW07C   10
17 Oct   CAESARS PALACE GP, Las Vegas
    A. Jones          Williams-Cosworth FW07C   1
    C. Reutemann Williams-Cosworth FW07C   8

# 1982

23 Jan   SOUTH AFRICAN GP, Kyalami
    C. Reutemann Williams-Cosworth FW07C   2
    K. Rosberg      Williams-Cosworth FW07C   5
21 Mar   BRAZILIAN GP, Rio de Janeiro
    C. Reutemann Williams-Cosworth FW07C   R
    * K. Rosberg  Williams-Cosworth FW07C   2
4 Apr    US GP WEST, Long Beach
    K. Rosberg      Williams-Cosworth FW07C   2
    M. Andretti   Williams-Cosworth FW07C   R
10 Apr   Race of Champions, Brands Hatch
    K. Rosberg      Williams-Cosworth FW08C   1
9 May    BELGIAN GP, Zolder
    K. Rosberg      Williams-Cosworth FW08   2
    D. Daly           Williams-Cosworth FW08   R

23 May   MONACO GP, Monte Carlo
    K. Rosberg      Williams-Cosworth FW08   R
    D. Daly           Williams-Cosworth FW08   6
6 Jun    UNITED STATES GP, Detroit
    K. Rosberg      Williams-Cosworth FW08   4
    D. Daly           Williams-Cosworth FW08   5
13 Jun   CANADIAN GP, Montreal
    K. Rosberg      Williams-Cosworth FW08   R
    D. Daly           Williams-Cosworth FW08   7
3 Jul    DUTCH GP, Zandvoort
    K. Rosberg      Williams-Cosworth FW08   3
    D. Daly           Williams-Cosworth FW08   5
18 Jul   BRITISH GP, Brands Hatch
    K. Rosberg      Williams-Cosworth FW08   R
    D. Daly           Williams-Cosworth FW08   5
25 Jul   FRENCH GP, Circuit Paul Ricard
    K. Rosberg      Williams-Cosworth FW08   5
    D. Daly           Williams-Cosworth FW08   7
8 Aug    GERMAN GP, Hockenheim
    K. Rosberg      Williams-Cosworth FW08   3
    D. Daly           Williams-Cosworth FW08   R
15 Aug   AUSTRIAN GP, Osterreichring
    K. Rosberg      Williams-Cosworth FW08   2
    D. Daly           Williams-Cosworth FW08   R
29 Aug   SWISS GP, Dijon-Prenois, France
    K. Rosberg      Williams-Cosworth FW08   1
    D. Daly           Williams-Cosworth FW08   9
12 Sep   ITALIAN GP, Monza
    K. Rosberg      Williams-Cosworth FW08   8
    D. Daly           Williams-Cosworth FW08   R
25 Sep   CAESARS PALACE GP, Las Vegas
    K. Rosberg      Williams-Cosworth FW08   5
    D. Daly           Williams-Cosworth FW08   6

*  later excluded

# 1983

13 Mar   BRAZILIAN GP, Rio de Janeiro
    * K. Rosberg  Williams-Cosworth FW08C   2
    J. Laffite        Williams-Cosworth FW08C   4
27 Mar   US GP WEST, Long Beach
    K. Rosberg      Williams-Cosworth FW08C   R
    J. Laffite        Williams-Cosworth FW08C   4
17 Apr   FRENCH GP, Circuit Paul Ricard
    K. Rosberg      Williams-Cosworth FW08C   5
    J. Laffite        Williams-Cosworth FW08C   6

1 May   SAN MARINO GP, Imola
K. Rosberg    Williams-Cosworth FW08C    4
J. Laffite    Williams-Cosworth FW08C    7
15 May   MONACO GP, Monte Carlo
K. Rosberg    Williams-Cosworth FW08C    1
J. Laffite    Williams-Cosworth FW08C    R
22 May   BELGIAN GP, Spa Francorchamps
K. Rosberg    Williams-Cosworth FW08C    5
J. Laffite    Williams-Cosworth FW08C    6
5 Jun   UNITED STATES GP, Detroit
K. Rosberg    Williams-Cosworth FW08C    2
J. Laffite    Williams-Cosworth FW08C    5
12 Jun   CANADIAN GP, Montreal
K. Rosberg    Williams-Cosworth FW08C    4
J. Laffite    Williams-Cosworth FW08C    R
16 Jul   BRITISH GP, Silverstone
K. Rosberg    Williams-Cosworth FW08C    11
J. Laffite    Williams-Cosworth FW08C    12
7 Aug   GERMAN GP, Hockenheim
K. Rosberg    Williams-Cosworth FW08C    10
J. Laffite    Williams-Cosworth FW08C    6
14 Aug   AUSTRIAN GP, Osterreichring
K. Rosberg    Williams-Cosworth FW08C    8
J. Laffite    Williams-Cosworth FW08C    R
28 Aug   DUTCH GP, Zandvoort
K. Rosberg    Williams-Cosworth FW08C    R
J. Laffite    Williams-Cosworth FW08C    R
11 Sep   ITALIAN GP, Monza
* K. Rosberg  Williams-Cosworth FW08C    11
J. Laffite    Williams-Cosworth FW08C    Q
25 Sep   GP OF EUROPE, Brands Hatch
K. Rosberg    Williams-Cosworth FW08C    R
J. Laffite    Williams-Cosworth FW08C    Q
J. Palmer     Williams-Cosworth FW08C    13
15 Oct   SOUTH AFRICAN GP, Kyalami
K. Rosberg    Williams-Honda FW09    5
J. Laffite    Williams-Honda FW09    R
*   finished ninth but penalised for infringement
    at the start

## 1984

25 Mar   BRAZILIAN GP, Rio de Janeiro
K. Rosberg    Williams-Honda FW09    2
J. Laffite    Williams-HondaFW09    R
7 Apr   SOUTH AFRICAN GP, Kyalami,
K. Rosberg    Williams-Honda FW09    R
J. Laffite    Williams-Honda FW09    R

29 Apr   BELGIAN GP, Zolder
K. Rosberg    Williams-Honda FW09    4
J. Laffite    Williams-Honda FW09    R
6 May   SAN MARINO GP, Imola
K. Rosberg    Williams-Honda FW09    R
J. Laffite    Williams-Honda FW09    R
20 May   FRENCH GP, Dijon-Prenois
K. Rosberg    Williams-Honda FW09    6
J. Laffite    Williams-Honda FW09    8
3 Jun   MONACO GP, Monte Carlo
K. Rosberg    Williams-Honda FW09    4
J. Laffite    Williams-Honda FW09    8
17 Jun   CANADIAN GP, Montreal
K. Rosberg    Williams-Honda FW09    R
J. Laffite    Williams-Honda FW09    R
24 Jun   UNITED STATES GP, Detroit
K. Rosberg    Williams-Honda FW09    R
J. Laffite    Williams-Honda FW09    5
8 Jul   UNITED STATES GP, Dallas
K. Rosberg    Williams-Honda FW09    1
J. Laffite    Williams-Honda FW09    4
22 Jul   BRITISH GP, Brands Hatch
K. Rosberg    Williams-Honda FW09B    R
J. Laffite    Williams-Honda FW09B    R
5 Aug   GERMAN GP, Hockenheim
K. Rosberg    Williams-Honda FW09B    R
J. Laffite    Williams-Honda FW09B    R
19 Aug   AUSTRIAN GP, Osterreichring
K. Rosberg    Williams-Honda FW09B    R
J. Laffite    Williams-Honda FW09B    R
26 Aug   DUTCH GP, Zandvoort
K. Rosberg    Williams-Honda FW09B    8
J. Laffite    Williams-Honda FW09B    R
9 Sep   ITALIAN GP, Monza
K. Rosberg    Williams-Honda FW09B    R
J. Laffite    Williams-Honda FW09B    R
7 Oct   GP OF EUROPE, Nurburgring
K. Rosberg    Williams-Honda FW09B    R
J. Laffite    Williams-Honda FW09B    R
21 Oct   PORTUGUESE GP, Estoril
K. Rosberg    Williams-Honda FW09B    R
J. Laffite    Williams-Honda FW09B    14

## 1985

7 Apr   BRAZILIAN GP, Rio de Janeiro
K. Rosberg    Williams-Honda FW10    R
N. Mansell    Williams-Honda FW10    R

21 Apr   PORTUGUESE GP, Estoril
K. Rosberg   Williams-Honda FW10   R
N. Mansell   Williams-Honda FW10   5

5 May   SAN MARINO GP, Imola
K. Rosberg   Williams-Honda FW10   R
N. Mansell   Williams-Honda FW10   5

19 May   MONACO GP, Monte Carlo
K. Rosberg   Williams-Honda FW10   8
N. Mansell   Williams-Honda FW10   7

16 Jun   CANADIAN GP, Montreal
K. Rosberg   Williams-Honda FW10   4
N. Mansell   Williams-Honda FW10   6

23 Jun   UNITED STATES GP, Detroit
K. Rosberg   Williams-Honda FW10   1
N. Mansell   Williams-Honda FW10   R

7 Jul   FRENCH GP, Circuit Paul Ricard
K. Rosberg   Williams-Honda FW10   2
N. Mansell   Williams-Honda FW10   N

21 Jul   BRITISH GP, Silverstone
K. Rosberg   Williams-Honda FW10   R
N. Mansell   Williams-Honda FW10   R

4 Aug   GERMAN GP, Nurburgring
K. Rosberg   Williams-Honda FW10   12
N. Mansell   Williams-Honda FW10   6

18 Aug   AUSTRIAN GP, Osterreichring
K. Rosberg   Williams-Honda FW10   R
N. Mansell   Williams-Honda FW10   R

25 Aug   DUTCH GP, Zandvoort
K. Rosberg   Williams-Honda FW10   R
N. Mansell   Williams-Honda FW10   6

8 Sep   ITALIAN GP, Monza
K. Rosberg   Williams-Honda FW10   R
N. Mansell   Williams-Honda FW10   11

15 Sep   BELGIAN GP, Spa Francorchamps
K. Rosberg   Williams-Honda FW10   4
N. Mansell   Williams-Honda FW10   2

6 Oct   GP OF EUROPE, Brands Hatch
K. Rosberg   Williams-Honda FW10   3
N. Mansell   Williams-Honda FW10   1

19 Oct   SOUTH AFRICAN GP, Kyalami
K. Rosberg   Williams-Honda FW10   2
N. Mansell   Williams-Honda FW10   1

3 Nov   AUSTRALIAN GP, Adelaide
K. Rosberg   Williams-Honda FW10   1
N. Mansell   Williams-Honda FW10   R

# 1986

23 Mar   BRAZILIAN GP, Rio de Janeiro
N. Mansell   Williams-Honda FW11   R
N. Piquet   Williams-Honda FW11   1

13 Apr   SPANISH GP, Jerez
N. Mansell   Williams-Honda FW11   2
N. Piquet   Williams-Honda FW11   R

27 Apr   SAN MARINO GP, Imola
N. Mansell   Williams-Honda FW11   R
N. Piquet   Williams-Honda FW11   2

11 May   MONACO GP, Monte Carlo
N. Mansell   Williams-Honda FW11   4
N. Piquet   Williams-Honda FW11   7

25 May   BELGIAN GP, Spa Francorchamps
N. Mansell   Williams-Honda FW11   1
N. Piquet   Williams-Honda FW11   R

15 Jun   CANADIAN GP, Montreal
N. Mansell   Williams-Honda FW11   1
N. Piquet   Williams-Honda FW11   3

22 Jun   UNITED STATES GP, Detroit
N. Mansell   Williams-Honda FW11   5
N. Piquet   Williams-Honda FW11   R

6 Jul   FRENCH GP, Circuit Paul Ricard
N. Mansell   Williams-Honda FW11   1
N. Piquet   Williams-Honda FW11   3

13 Jul   BRITISH GP, Brands Hatch
N. Mansell   Williams-Honda FW11   1
N. Piquet   Williams-Honda FW11   2

27 Jul   GERMAN GP, Hockenheim
N. Mansell   Williams-Honda FW11   3
N. Piquet   Williams-Honda FW11   1

10 Aug   HUNGARIAN GP, Hungaroring
N. Mansell   Williams-Honda FW11   3
N. Piquet   Williams-Honda FW11   1

17 Aug   AUSTRIAN GP, Osterreichring
N. Mansell   Williams-Honda FW11   R
N. Piquet   Williams-Honda FW11   R

7 Sep   ITALIAN GP, Monza
N. Mansell   Williams-Honda FW11   2
N. Piquet   Williams-Honda FW11   1

21 Sep   PORTUGUESE GP, Estoril
N. Mansell   Williams-Honda FW11   1
N. Piquet   Williams-Honda FW11   3

12 Oct   MEXICAN GP, Mexico City
N. Mansell   Williams-Honda FW11   5
N. Piquet   Williams-Honda FW11   4

26 Oct   AUSTRALIAN GP, Adelaide
N. Mansell   Williams-Honda FW11        R
N. Piquet    Williams-Honda FW11        2

# 1987

12 Apr   BRAZILIAN GP, Rio de Janeiro
N. Mansell   Williams-Honda FW11B       6
N. Piquet    Williams-Honda FW11B       2
3 May   SAN MARINO GP, Imola
N. Mansell   Williams-Honda FW11B       1
N. Piquet    Williams-Honda FW11B       N
17 May   BELGIAN GP, Spa Francorchamps
N. Mansell   Williams-Honda FW11B       R
N. Piquet    Williams-Honda FW11B       R
31 May   MONACO GP, Monte Carlo
N. Mansell   Williams-Honda FW11B       R
N. Piquet    Williams-Honda FW11B       2
21 Jun   UNITED STATES GP, Detroit
N. Mansell   Williams-Honda FW11B       5
N. Piquet    Williams-Honda FW11B       2
5 Jul    FRENCH GP, Circuit Paul Ricard
N. Mansell   Williams-Honda FW11B       1
N. Piquet    Williams-Honda FW11B       2
12 Jul   BRITISH GP, Silverstone
N. Mansell   Williams-Honda FW11B       1
N. Piquet    Williams-Honda FW11B       2
26 Jul   GERMAN GP, Hockenheim
N. Mansell   Williams-Honda FW11B       R
N. Piquet    Williams-Honda FW11B       1
9 Aug   HUNGARIAN GP, Hungaroring
N. Mansell   Williams-Honda FW11B       14
N. Piquet    Williams-Honda FW11B       1
16 Aug   AUSTRIAN GP, Osterreichring
N. Mansell   Williams-Honda FW11B       1
N. Piquet    Williams-Honda FW11B       2
6 Sep    ITALIAN GP, Monza
N. Mansell   Williams-Honda FW11B       3
N. Piquet    Williams-Honda FW11B       1
20 Sep   PORTUGUESE GP, Estoril
N. Mansell   Williams-Honda FW11B       R
N. Piquet    Williams-Honda FW11B       3
27 Sep   SPANISH GP, Jerez
N. Mansell   Williams-Honda FW11B       1
N. Piquet    Williams-Honda FW11B       4
18 Oct   MEXICAN GP, Mexico City
N. Mansell   Williams-Honda FW11B       1
N. Piquet    Williams-Honda FW11B       2

1 Nov   JAPANESE GP, Suzuka
N. Mansell   Williams-Honda FW11B       N
N. Piquet    Williams-Honda FW11B       R
15 Nov   AUSTRALIAN GP, Adelaide
R. Patrese   Williams-Honda FW11B       R
N. Piquet    Williams-Honda FW11B       R

# 1988

3 Apr    BRAZILIAN GP, Rio de Janeiro
N. Mansell   Williams-Judd FW12         R
R. Patrese   Williams-Judd FW12         R
1 May    SAN MARINO GP, Imola
N. Mansell   Williams-Judd FW12         R
R. Patrese   Williams-Judd FW12         13
15 May   MONACO GP, Monte Carlo
N. Mansell   Williams-Judd FW12         R
R. Patrese   Williams-Judd FW12         6
29 May   MEXICAN GP, Mexico City
N. Mansell   Williams-Judd FW12         R
R. Patrese   Williams-Judd FW12         R
12 Jun   CANADIAN GP, Montreal
N. Mansell   Williams-Judd FW12         R
R. Patrese   Williams-Judd FW12         R
19 Jun   UNITED STATES GP, Detroit
N. Mansell   Williams-Judd FW12         R
R. Patrese   Williams-Judd FW12         R
3 Jul    FRENCH GP, Circuit Paul Ricard
N. Mansell   Williams-Judd FW12         R
R. Patrese   Williams-Judd FW12         R
10 Jul   BRITISH GP, Silverstone
N. Mansell   Williams-Judd FW12         2
R. Patrese   Williams-Judd FW12         8
24 Jul   GERMAN GP, Hockenheim
N. Mansell   Williams-Judd FW12         R
R. Patrese   Williams-Judd FW12         R
7 Aug    HUNGARIAN GP, Hungaroring
N. Mansell   Williams-Judd FWl2         R
R. Patrese   Williams-Judd FW12         6
28 Aug   BELGIAN GP, Spa Francorchamps
M. Brundle   Williams-Judd FW12         7
R. Patrese   Williams-Judd FW12         R
11 Sep   ITALIAN GP, Monza
J-L. Schlesser Williams-Judd FW12       11
R. Patrese   Williams-Judd FW12         7
25 Sep   PORTUGUESE GP, Estoril
N. Mansell   Williams-Judd FW12         R
R. Patrese   Williams-Judd FW12         R

2 Oct   SPANISH GP, Jerez
  N. Mansell   Williams-Judd FW12   2
  R. Patrese   Williams-Judd FW12   5
30 Oct   JAPANESE GP, Suzuka
  N. Mansell   Williams-Judd FW12   R
  R. Patrese   Williams-Judd FW12   6
13 Nov   AUSTRALIAN GP, Adelaide
  N. Mansell   Williams-Judd FW12   R
  R. Patrese   Williams-Judd FW12   4

# 1989

26 Mar   BRAZILIAN GP, Rio de Janeiro
  T. Boutsen   Williams-Renault FW12C   R
  R. Patrese   Williams-Renault FW12C   R
23 Apr   SAN MARINO GP, Imola
  T. Boutsen   Williams-Renault FW12C   4
  R. Patrese   Williams-Renault FW12C   R
7 May   MONACO GP, Monte Carlo
  T. Boutsen   Williams-Renault FW12C   10
  R. Patrese   Williams-Renault FW12C   15
28 May   MEXICAN GP, Mexico City
  T. Boutsen   Williams-Renault FW12C   R
  R. Patrese   Williams-Renault FW12C   2
4 Jun   UNITED STATES GP, Phoenix
  T. Boutsen   Williams-Renault FW12C   6
  R. Patrese   Williams-Renault FW12C   2
18 Jun   CANADIAN GP, Montreal
  T. Boutsen   Williams-Renault FW12C   1
  R. Patrese   Williams-Renault FW12C   2
9 Jul   FRENCH GP, Circuit Paul Ricard
  T. Boutsen   Williams-Renault FW12C   R
  R. Patrese   Williams-Renault FW12C   3
16 Jul   BRITISH GP, Silverstone
  T. Boutsen   Williams-Renault FW12C   10
  R. Patrese   Williams-Renault FW12C   R
30 Jul   GERMAN GP, Hockenheim
  T. Boutsen   Williams-Renault FW12C   R
  R. Patrese   Williams-Renault FW12C   4
13 Aug   HUNGARIAN GP, Hungaroring
  T. Boutsen   Williams-Renault FW12C   3
  R. Patrese   Williams-Renault FW12C   R
27 Aug   BELGIAN GP, Spa Francorchamps
  T. Boutsen   Williams-Renault FW12C   4
  R. Patrese   Williams-Renault FW12C   R
10 Sep   ITALIAN GP, Monza
  T. Boutsen   Williams-Renault FW12C   3
  R. Patrese   Williams-Renault FW12C   4

24 Sep   PORTUGUESE GP, Estoril
  T. Boutsen   Williams-Renault FW13   R
  R. Patrese   Williams-Renault FW13   R
1 Oct   SPANISH GP, Jerez
  T. Boutsen   Williams-Renault FW13   R
  R. Patrese   Williams-Renault FW12C   5
22 Oct   JAPANESE GP, Suzuka
  T. Boutsen   Williams-Renault FW13   3
  R. Patrese   Williams-Renault FW13   2
5 Nov   AUSTRALIAN GP, Adelaide
  T. Boutsen   Williams-Renault FW13   1
  R. Patrese   Williams-Renault FW13   3

# 1990

11 Mar   UNITED STATES GP, Phoenix
  T. Boutsen   Williams-Renault FW13B   3
  R. Patrese   Williams-Renault FW13B   9
25 Mar   BRAZILIAN GP, Interlagos
  T. Boutsen   Williams-Renault FW13B   5
  R. Patrese   Williams-Renault FW13B   13
13 May   SAN MARINO GP, Imola
  T. Boutsen   Williams-Renault FW13B   R
  R. Patrese   Williams-Renault FW13B   1
27 May   MONACO GP, Monte Carlo
  T. Boutsen   Williams-Renault FW13B   4
  R. Patrese   Williams-Renault FW13B   R
10 Jun   CANADIAN GP, Montreal
  T. Boutsen   Williams-Renault FW13B   R
  R. Patrese   Williams-Renault FW13B   R
24 Jun   MEXICAN GP, Mexico City
  T. Boutsen   Williams-Renault FW13B   5
  R. Patrese   Williams-Renault FW13B   9
8 Jul   FRENCH GP, Circuit Paul Ricard
  T. Boutsen   Williams-Renault FW13B   R
  R. Patrese   Williams-Renault FW13B   6
15 Jul   BRITISH GP, Silverstone
  T. Boutsen   Williams-Renault FW13B   2
  R. Patrese   Williams-Renault FW13B   R
29 Jul   GERMAN GP, Hockenheim
  T. Boutsen   Williams-Renault FW13B   6
  R. Patrese   Williams-Renault FW13B   5
12 Aug   HUNGARIAN GP, Hungaroring
  T. Boutsen   Williams-Renault FW13B   1
  R. Patrese   Williams-Renault FW13B   4
26 Aug   BELGIAN GP, Spa Francorchamps
  T. Boutsen   Williams-Renault FW13B   R
  R. Patrese   Williams-Renault FW13B   R

9 Sep   ITALIAN GP, Monza
T. Boutsen   Williams-Renault FW13B   R
R. Patrese   Williams-Renault FW13B   5
23 Sep   PORTUGUESE GP, Estoril
T. Boutsen   Williams-Renault FW13B   R
R. Patrese   Williams-Renault FW13B   7
30 Sep   SPANISH GP, Jerez
T. Boutsen   Williams-Renault FW13B   4
R. Patrese   Williams-Renault FW13B   5
21 Oct   JAPANESE GP, Suzuka
T. Boutsen   Williams-Renault FW13B   5
R. Patrese   Williams-Renault FW13B   4
4 Nov   AUSTRALIAN GP, Adelaide
T. Boutsen   Williams-Renault FW13B   5
R. Patrese   Williams-Renault FW13B   6

# 1991

10 Mar   UNITED STATES GP, Phoenix
N. Mansell   Williams-Renault FW14   R
R. Patrese   Williams-Renault FW14   R
24 Mar   BRAZILIAN GP, Interlagos
N. Mansell   Williams-Renault FW14   R
R. Patrese   Williams-Renault FW14   2
28 Apr   SAN MARINO GP, Imola
N. Mansell   Williams-Renault FW14   R
R. Patrese   Williams-Renault FW14   R
12 May   MONACO GP, Monte Carlo
N. Mansell   Williams-Renault FW14   2
R. Patrese   Williams-Renault FW14   R
2 Jun   CANADIAN GP, Montreal
N. Mansell   Williams-Renault FW14   6
R. Patrese   Williams-Renault FW14   3
16 Jun   MEXICAN GP, Mexico City
N. Mansell   Williams-Renault FW14   2
R. Patrese   Williams-Renault FW14   1
7 Jul   FRENCH GP, Magny-Cours
N. Mansell   Williams-Renault FW14   1
R. Patrese   Williams-Renault FW14   5
14 Jul   BRITISH GP, Silverstone
N. Mansell   Williams-Renault FW14   1
R. Patrese   Williams-Renault FW14   R
28 Jul   GERMAN GP, Hockenheim
N. Mansell   Williams-Renault FW14   1
R. Patrese   Williams-Renault FW14   2
11 Aug   HUNGARIAN GP, Budapest
N. Mansell   Williams-Renault FW14   2
R. Patrese   Williams-Renault FW14   3

25 Aug   BELGIAN GP, Spa Francorchamps
N. Mansell   Williams-Renault FW14   R
R. Patrese   Williams-Renault FW14   5
8 Sep   ITALIAN GP, Monza
N. Mansell   Williams-Renault FW14   1
R. Patrese   Williams-Renault FW14   R
22 Sep   PORTUGUESE GP, Estoril
N. Mansell   Williams-Renault FW14   D
R. Patrese   Williams-Renault FW14   1
29 Sep   SPANISH GP, Barcelona
N. Mansell   Williams-Renault FW14   1
R. Patrese   Williams-Renault FW14   3
20 Oct   JAPANESE GP, Suzuka
N. Mansell   Williams-Renault FW14   R
R. Patrese   Williams-Renault FW14   3
3 Nov   AUSTRALIAN GP, Adelaide
N. Mansell   Williams-Renault FW14   R
R. Patrese   Williams-Renault FW14   5

# 1992

1 Mar   SOUTH AFRICAN GP, Kyalami
N. Mansell   Williams-Renault FW14B   1
R. Patrese   Williams-Renault FW14B   2
22 Mar   MEXICAN GP, Mexico City
N. Mansell   Williams-Renault FW14B   1
R. Patrese   Williams-Renault FW14B   2
5 Apr   BRAZILIAN GP, Interlagos
N. Mansell   Williams-Renault FW14B   1
R. Patrese   Williams-Renault FW14B   2
3 May   SPANISH GP, Barcelona
N. Mansell   Williams-Renault FW14B   1
R. Patrese   Williams-Renault FW14B   R
17 May   SAN MARINO GP, Imola
N. Mansell   Williams-Renault FW14B   1
R. Patrese   Williams-Renault FW14B   2
31 May   MONACO GP, Monte Carlo
N. Mansell   Williams-Renault FW14B   2
R. Patrese   Williams-Renault FW14B   3
14 Jun   CANADIAN GP, Montreal
N. Mansell   Williams-Renault FW14B   R
R. Patrese   Williams-Renault FW14B   R
5 Jul   FRENCH GP, Magny-Cours
N. Mansell   Williams-Renault FW14B   1
R. Patrese   Williams-Renault FW14B   2
12 Jul   BRITISH GP, Silverstone
N. Mansell   Williams-Renault FW14B   1
R. Patrese   Williams-Renault FW14B   2

26 Jul    GERMAN GP, Hockenheim
N. Mansell    Williams-Renault FW14B    1
R. Patrese    Williams-Renault FW14B    8
16 Aug    HUNGARIAN GP, Budapest
N. Mansell    Williams-Renault FW14B    2
R. Patrese    Williams-Renault FW14B    R
30 Aug    BELGIAN GP, Spa-Francorchamps
N. Mansell    Williams-Renault FW14B    2
R. Patrese    Williams-Renault FW14B    3
13 Sep    ITALIAN GP, Monza
N. Mansell    Williams-Renault FW14B    R
R. Patrese    Williams-Renault FW14B    5
27 Sep    PORTUGUESE GP, Estoril
N. Mansell    Williams-Renault FW14B    1
R. Patrese    Williams-Renault FW14B    R
25 Oct    JAPANESE GP, Suzuka
N. Mansell    Williams-Renault FW14B    R
R. Patrese    Williams-Renault FW14B    1
8 Nov    AUSTRALIAN GP, Adelaide
N. Mansell    Williams-Renault FW14B    R
R. Patrese    Williams-Renault FW14B    R

# 1993

14 Mar    SOUTH AFRICAN GP, Kyalami
A. Prost    Williams-Renault FW15C    1
D. Hill    Williams-Renault FW15C    R
28 Mar    BRAZILIAN GP, Interlagos
A. Prost    Williams-Renault FW15C    R
D. Hill    Williams-Renault FW15C    2
11 Apr    EUROPEAN GP, Donington Park
A. Prost    Williams-Renault FW15C    3
D. Hill    Williams-Renault FW15C    2
25 Apr    SAN MARINO GP, Imola
A. Prost    Williams-Renault FW15C    1
D. Hill    Williams-Renault FW15C    R
9 May    SPANISH GP, Barcelona
A. Prost    Williams-Renault FW15C    1
D. Hill    Williams-Renault FW15C    R
23 May    MONACO GP, Monte Carlo
A. Prost    Williams-Renault FW15C    4
D. Hill    Williams-Renault FW15C    2
13 Jun    CANADIAN GP, Montreal
A. Prost    Williams-Renault FW15C    1
D. Hill    Williams-Renault FW15C    3
4 Jul    FRENCH GP, Magny-Cours
A. Prost    Williams-Renault FW15C    1
D. Hill    Williams-Renault FW15C    2

11 Jul    BRITISH GP, Silverstone
A. Prost    Williams-Renault FW15C    1
D. Hill    Williams-Renault FW15C    R
25 Jul    GERMAN GP, Hockenheim
A. Prost    Williams-Renault FW15C    1
D. Hill    Williams-Renault FW15C    R
15 Aug    HUNGARIAN GP, Budapest
A. Prost    Williams-Renault FW15C    12
D. Hill    Williams-Renault FW15C    1
29 Aug    BELGIAN GP, Spa-Francorchamps
A. Prost    Williams-Renault FW15C    3
D. Hill    Williams-Renault FW15C    1
12 Sep    ITALIAN GP, Monza
A. Prost    Williams-Renault FW15C    R
D. Hill    Williams-Renault FW15C    1
26 Sep    PORTUGUESE GP, Estoril
A. Prost    Williams-Renault FW15C    2
D. Hill    Williams-Renault FW15C    3
24 Oct    JAPANESE GP, Suzuka
A. Prost    Williams-Renault FW15C    2
D. Hill    Williams-Renault FW15C    4
7 Nov    AUSTRALIAN GP, Adelaide
A. Prost    Williams-Renault FW15C    2
D. Hill    Williams-Renault FW15C    3

# 1994

27 Mar    BRAZILIAN GP, Interlagos
A. Senna    Williams-Renault FW16    R
D. Hill    Williams-Renault FW16    2
17 Apr    PACIFIC GP, Aida
A. Senna    Williams-Renault FW16    R
D. Hill    Williams-Renault FW16    R
1 May    SAN MARINO GP, Imola
A. Senna    Williams-Renault FW16    F
D. Hill    Williams-Renault FW16    6
15 May    MONACO GP, Monte Carlo
D. Hill    Williams-Renault FW16    R
29 May    SPANISH GP, Barcelona
D. Hill    Williams-Renault FW16    1
D. Coulthard Williams-Renault FW16    R
12 Jun    CANADIAN GP, Montreal
D. Hill    Williams-Renault FW16    2
D. Coulthard Williams-Renault FW16    5
3 Jul    FRENCH GP, Magny-Cours
D. Hill    Williams-Renault FW16    2
N. Mansell    Williams-Renault FW16    R

10 Jul    BRITISH GP, Silverstone
    D. Hill        Williams-Renault FW16    1
    D. Coulthard Williams-Renault FW16    5
31 Jul    GERMAN GP, Hockenheim
    D. Hill        Williams-Renault FW16B    8
    D. Coulthard Williams-Renault FW16B    R
14 Aug    HUNGARIAN GP, Budapest
    D. Hill        Williams-Renault FW16B    2
    D. Coulthard Williams-Renault FW16B    R
28 Aug    BELGIAN GP, Spa-Francorchamps
    D. Hill        Williams-Renault FW16B    1
    D. Coulthard Williams-Renault FW16B    4
11 Sep    ITALIAN GP, Monza
    D. Hill        Williams-Renault FW16B    1
    D. Coulthard Williams-Renault FW16B    6
25 Sep    PORTUGUESE GP, Estoril
    D. Hill        Williams-Renault FW16B    1
    D. Coulthard Williams-Renault FW16B    2
16 Oct    EUROPEAN GP, Jerez
    D. Hill        Williams-Renault FW16B    2
    N. Mansell   Williams-Renault FW16B    R
6 Nov    JAPANESE GP, Suzuka
    D. Hill        Williams-Renault FW16B    1
    N. Mansell   Williams-Renault FW16B    4
13 Nov    AUSTRALIAN GP, Adelaide
    D. Hill        Williams-Renault FW16B    R
    N. Mansell   Williams-Renault FW16B    1

# 1995

26 Mar    BRAZILIAN GP, Interlagos
    D. Hill        Williams-Renault FW17    R
    D. Coulthard Williams-Renault FW17    2
9 Apr    ARGENTINE GP, Buenos Aires
    D. Hill        Williams-Renault FW17    1
    D. Coulthard Williams-Renault FW17    R
30 Apr    SAN MARINO GP, Imola
    D. Hill        Williams-Renault FW17    1
    D. Coulthard Williams-Renault FW17    4
14 May    SPANISH GP, Barcelona
    D. Hill        Williams-Renault FW17    4
    D. Coulthard Williams-Renault FW17    R
28 May    MONACO GP, Monte Carlo
    D. Hill        Williams-Renault FW17    2
    D. Coulthard Williams-Renault FW17    R
11 Jun    CANADIAN GP, Montreal
    D. Hill        Williams-Renault FW17    R
    D. Coulthard Williams-Renault FW17    R

2 Jul    FRENCH GP, Magny-Cours
    D. Hill        Williams-Renault FW17    2
    D. Coulthard Williams-Renault FW17    3
16 Jul    BRITISH GP, Silverstone
    D. Hill        Williams-Renault FW17    R
    D. Coulthard Williams-Renault FW17    3
30 Jul    GERMAN GP, Hockenheim
    D. Hill        Williams-Renault FW17    R
    D. Coulthard Williams-Renault FW17    2
13 Aug    HUNGARIAN GP, Budapest
    D. Hill        Williams-Renault FW17    1
    D. Coulthard Williams-Renault FW17    2
27 Aug    BELGIAN GP, Spa-Francorchamps
    D. Hill        Williams-Renault FW17    2
    D. Coulthard Williams-Renault FW17    R
10 Sep    ITALIAN GP, Monza
    D. Hill        Williams-Renault FW17    R
    D. Coulthard Williams-Renault FW17    R
24 Sep    PORTUGUESE GP, Estoril
    D. Hill        Williams-Renault FW17    3
    D. Coulthard Williams-Renault FW17    1
1 Oct    EUROPEAN GP, Nurburgring
    D. Hill        Williams-Renault FW17B    R
    D. Coulthard Williams-Renault FW17B    3
22 Oct    PACIFIC GP, Aida
    D. Hill        Williams-Renault FW17B    3
    D. Coulthard Williams-Renault FW17B    2
29 Oct    JAPANESE GP, Suzuka.
    D. Hill        Williams-Renault FW17B    R
    D. Coulthard Williams-Renault FW17B    R
12 Nov    AUSTRALIAN GP, Adelaide
    D. Hill        Williams-Renault FW17B    1
    D. Coulthard Willams-Renault FW17B    R

# 1996

10 Mar    AUSTRALIAN GP, Melbourne
    D. Hill        Williams-Renault FW18    1
    J. Villeneuve Williams-Renault FW18    2
31 Mar    BRAZILIAN GP, Interlagos
    D. Hill        Williams-Renault FW18    1
    J. Villeneuve Williams-Renault FW18    R
7 Apr    ARGENTINE GP, Buenos Aires
    D. Hill        Williams-Renault FW18    1
    J. Villeneuve Williams-Renault FW18    2
28 Apr    EUROPEAN GP, Nurburgring
    D. Hill        Williams-Renault FW18    4
    J. Villeneuve Williams-Renault FW18    1

| | | | |
|---|---|---|---|
| 5 May   SAN MARINO GP, Imola | | 7 Apr   ARGENTINE GP, Buenos Aires | |
| D. Hill        Williams-Renault FW18 | 1 | J. Villeneuve  Williams-Renault FW19 | 1 |
| J. Villeneuve  Williams-Renault FW18 | R | H.H. Frentzen Williams-Renault FW19 | R |
| 19 May   MONACO GP, Monte Carlo | | 27 Apr   SAN MARINO GP, Imola | |
| D. Hill        Williams-Renault FW18 | R | J. Villeneuve  Williams-Renault FW19 | R |
| J. Villeneuve  Williams-Renault FW18 | R | H.H. Frentzen Williams-Renault FW19 | 1 |
| 2 Jun   SPANISH GP, Barcelona | | 11 May   MONACO GP, Monte Carlo | |
| D. Hill        Williams-Renault FW18 | R | J. Villeneuve  Williams-Renault FW19 | R |
| J. Villeneuve  Williams-Renault FW18 | 3 | H.H. Frentzen Williams-Renault FW19 | R |
| 16 Jun   CANADIAN GP, Montreal | | 25 May   SPANISH GP, Barcelona | |
| D. Hill        Williams-Renault FW18 | 1 | J. Villeneuve  Williams-Renault FW19 | 1 |
| J. Villeneuve  Williams-Renault FW18 | 2 | H.H. Frentzen Williams-Renault FW19 | 8 |
| 30 Jun   FRENCH GP, Magny-Cours | | 15 Jun   CANADIAN GP, Montreal | |
| D. Hill        Williams-Renault FW18 | 1 | J. Villeneuve  Williams-Renault FW19 | R |
| J. Villeneuve  Williams-Renault FW18 | 2 | H.H. Frentzen Williams-Renault FW19 | 4 |
| 14 Jul   BRITISH GP, Silverstone | | 29 Jun   FRENCH GP, Magny-Cours | |
| D. Hill        Williams-Renault FW18 | R | J. Villeneuve  Williams-Renault FW19 | 4 |
| J. Villeneuve  Williams-Renault FW18 | 1 | H.H. Frentzen Williams-Renault FW19 | 2 |
| 28 Jul   GERMAN GP, Hockenheim | | 13 Jul   BRITISH GP, Silverstone | |
| D. Hill        Williams-Renault FW18 | 1 | J. Villeneuve  Williams-Renault FW19 | 1 |
| J. Villeneuve  Williams-Renault FW18 | 3 | H.H. Frentzen Williams-Renault FW19 | R |
| 11 Aug   HUNGARIAN GP, Budapest | | 27 Jul   GERMAN GP, Hockenheim | |
| D. Hill        Williams-Renault FW18 | 2 | J. Villeneuve  Williams-Renault FW19 | R |
| J. Villeneuve  Williams-Renault FW18 | 1 | H.H. Frentzen Williams-Renault FW19 | R |
| 25 Aug   BELGIAN GP, Spa-Francorchamps | | 10 Aug   HUNGARIAN GP, Budapest | |
| D. Hill        Williams-Renault FW18 | 5 | J. Villeneuve  Williams-Renault FW19 | 1 |
| J. Villeneuve  Williams-Renault FW18 | 2 | H.H. Frentzen Williams-Renault FW19 | R |
| 8 Sep   ITALIAN GP, Monza | | 24 Aug   BELGIAN GP, Spa-Francorchamps | |
| D. Hill        Williams-Renault FW18 | R | J. Villeneuve  Williams-Renault FW19 | 5 |
| J. Villeneuve  Williams-Renault FW18 | 7 | H.H. Frentzen Williams-Renault FW19 | 3 |
| 22 Sep   PORTUGUESE GP, Estoril | | 7 Sep   ITALIAN GP, Monza | |
| D. Hill        Williams-Renault FW18 | 2 | J. Villeneuve  Williams-Renault FW19 | 5 |
| J. Villeneuve  Williams-Renault FW18 | 1 | H.H. Frentzen Williams-Renault FW19 | 3 |
| 13 Oct   JAPANESE GP, Suzuka | | 21 Sep   AUSTRIAN GP, A1-Ring | |
| D. Hill        Williams-Renault FW18 | 1 | J. Villeneuve  Williams-Renault FW19 | 1 |
| J. Villeneuve  Williams-Renault FW18 | R | H.H. Frentzen Williams-Renault FW19 | 3 |
| | | 28 Sep   LUXEMBOURG GP, Nurburgring | |
| | | J. Villeneuve  Williams-Renault FW19 | 1 |
| **1997** | | H.H. Frentzen Williams-Renault FW19 | 3 |
| | | 12 Oct   JAPANESE GP, Suzuka | |
| 9 Mar   AUSTRALIAN GP, Melbourne | | J. Villeneuve  Williams-Renault FW19 | D |
| J. Villeneuve  Williams-Renault FW19 | R | H.H. Frentzen Williams-Renault FW19 | 2 |
| H.H. Frentzen Williams-Renault FW19 | 8 | 26 Oct   EUROPEAN GP, Jerez | |
| 30 Mar   BRAZILIAN GP, Interlagos | | J. Villeneuve  Williams-Renault FW19 | 3 |
| J. Villeneuve  Williams-Renault FW19 | 1 | H.H. Frentzen Williams-Renault FW19 | 6 |
| H.H. Frentzen Williams-Renault FW19 | 9 | | |

# Appendix 2

# Williams –
# team statistics

RECORD TO END OF 1997:
(from 1973 when first built
cars under own name)

Grands Prix contested: 379
Pole positions: 108
Victories: 103
Fastest race laps: 109

CONSTRUCTORS'
CHAMPIONSHIP PLACINGS:

| | | | |
|---|---|---|---|
| 1973 | – | 10th | 2 points |
| 1974 | – | 10th | 4 points |
| 1975 | – | 9th | 6 points |
| 1976 | – | | 0 points |
| 1977 | – | | 0 points |
| 1978 | – | 9th | 11 points |
| 1979 | – | 2nd | 75 points |
| 1980 | – | 1st | 120 points |
| 1981 | – | 1st | 95 points |
| 1982 | – | 4th | 58 points |
| 1983 | – | 4th | 38 points |
| 1984 | – | 6th | 25.5 points |
| 1985 | – | 3rd | 71 points |
| 1986 | – | 1st | 141 points |
| 1987 | – | 1st | 137 points |
| 1988 | – | 7th | 20 points |
| 1989 | – | 2nd | 77 points |
| 1990 | – | 4th | 57 points |
| 1991 | – | 2nd | 125 points |
| 1992 | – | 1st | 164 points |
| 1993 | – | 1st | 168 points |
| 1994 | – | 1st | 118 points |
| 1995 | – | 2nd | 112 points |
| 1996 | – | 1st | 175 points |
| 1997 | – | 1st | 123 points |

# Appendix 3

# Williams – most successful drivers

NIGEL MANSELL (GB). Born 8.8.53. F1 debut, 1980, Austria (Lotus). Drove for Williams 1985–88, 91–92 and 94. 31 career wins, 28 for Williams. World Champion, 1992.

DAMON HILL (GB). Born 17.9.60. F1 debut, 1992, Britain (Brabham). Drove for Williams 1993–96. 21 career wins, all with Williams. World Champion 1996.

NELSON PIQUET (BR). Born 17.8.52. F1 debut, 1978, German (Ensign). Drove for Williams 1986 and 87. 23 career wins, seven with Williams. World Champion 1981 and 83 (Brabham) and 1987 (Williams).

ALAIN PROST (F). Born 24.2.55. F1 debut, 1980 Argentina (McLaren). Drove for Williams 1993. 51 career wins, seven for Williams. World Champion 1985, 86 and 89 (McLaren) and 1993 (Williams).

ALAN JONES (AUS). Born 2.11.46. F1 debut, 1975, Spain (Hesketh). Drove for Williams 1978–81. 12 career wins, 11 with Williams. World Champion 1980.

JACQUES VILLENEUVE (CDN). Born 9.4.71. F1 debut, 1996, Australia (Williams). Drove for Williams 1996 to date. 11 career wins, all with Williams. World Champion 1997.

KEKE ROSBERG (FIN). Born 6.12.48. F1 debut, 1978, South Africa (Theodore). Drove for Williams 1982–85. Five career wins, all for Williams. World Champion 1982.

RICCARDO PATRESE (I). Born 17.4.54. F1 debut, 1977, Monaco (Shadow). Drove for Williams 1987 (one race), then 1988–92. Six career wins, four for Williams.

CARLOS REUTEMANN (ARG). Born 12.4.42. F1 debut, 1972, Argentina (Brabham). Drove for Williams: 1980–82. 12 career wins, three for Williams.

HEINZ-HARALD FRENTZEN (D). Born 18.5.67. F1 debut, 1994, Brazil (Sauber). Drove for Williams 1997 to date. 1 career win, with Williams.

# OTHER BOOKS OF INTEREST

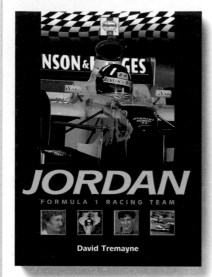

### JORDAN
FORMULA 1 RACING TEAM

David Tremayne

### JACQUES VILLENEUVE
Champion of two worlds

CHRISTOPHER HILTON

### HEINZ-HARALD FRENTZEN
Back on the pace

CHRISTOPHER HILTON

### MICHAEL SCHUMACHER
Controversial genius

CHRISTOPHER HILTON

**AUDIO CASSETTES** A collection of audio cassettes featuring top Formula 1 drivers is available from **Audiosport Ltd**, The Fairway, Bush Fair, Harlow, Essex CM18 6LY (tel: 01279 444707). Scripted by Christopher Hilton and narrated by Julian Harries, the Grand Prix Heroes series includes cassettes on Jacques Villeneuve, Michael Schumacher, Mika Hakkinen and Johnny Herbert.

For more information on books please contact: Customer Services, Haynes Publishing, Sparkford, Nr Yeovil, Somerset BA22 7JJ
Tel. 01963 440635 Fax: 01963 440001
Int. tel: +44 1963 440635 Fax: +44 1963 440001
E-mail: sales@haynes-manuals.co.uk Web site: http://www.haynes.com

Haynes
THE BOOK

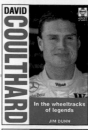

### DAVID COULTHARD
In the wheeltracks of legends

JIM DUNN

### MIKA HAKKINEN
Doing what comes naturally

CHRISTOPHER HILTON

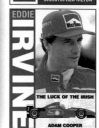

### EDDIE IRVINE
THE LUCK OF THE IRISH

ADAM COOPER

### JOHNNY HERBERT
THE STEEL BEHIND THE SMILE

CHRISTOPHER HILTON

### JEAN ALESI
BEATING THE ODDS

Christopher Hilton

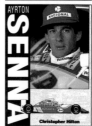

### AYRTON SENNA

Christopher Hilton

### COLIN McRAE
Rallying's fast master

DAVID WILLIAMS